SHARING
THE
WEIGHT
OF
Grief

SHARING THE WEIGHT OF *Grief*

Dr. Jacqueline L. Phelps

SHARING THE WEIGHT OF GRIEF
Copyright © 2021 Jacqueline L. Phelps
All rights reserved.

Published by Publish Your Gift®
An imprint of Purposely Created Publishing Group, LLC

No part of this book may be reproduced, distributed or transmitted in any form by any means, graphic, electronic, or mechanical, including photocopy, recording, taping, or by any information storage or retrieval system, without permission in writing from the publisher, except in the case of reprints in the context of reviews, quotes, or references.

Printed in the United States of America

ISBN: 978-1-64484-359-8 (print)
ISBN: 978-1-64484-360-4 (ebook)

Special discounts are available on bulk quantity purchases by book clubs, associations and special interest groups. For details email: sales@publishyourgift.com or call (888) 949-6228.
For information log on to www.PublishYourGift.com

Table of Contents

Acknowledgments vii

Introduction 1

   Called to Service 2

   Deeper Look at Principle 1: The Work Belongs to God 28

   Deeper Look at Principle 2: Silence Is More than Okay, It Is Vital 35

   Deeper Look at Principle 3: The Holy Spirit Is the Master Teacher 39

   Deeper Look at Principle 4: The Journey Belongs to Your Grieving Loved One 40

Chapter 1: Shock 45

Chapter 2: Denial 57

Chapter 3: Anger 81

Chapter 4: Guilt 107

Chapter 5: Depression 117

Chapter 6: Acceptance 137

Chapter 7: Engaging in Life 147

Quick Reference Guide 163

References 207

About the Author 211

Acknowledgments

I would like to start by acknowledging my inspiration and hope—Juanita Gannaway Agnew—the grandmother I never had the privilege of meeting because she passed over from tuberculosis when my mother was only two years old. The amazing stories of her life and fight to stand tall as a young black woman in the South have served as an inspiration to me. Her battle and ultimate eternal victory over tuberculosis. The loneliness and agony of being in forced isolation due to community quarantines, away from her husband, my grandfather, John Willey Agnew Sr., and her two baby girls. She lived the last of her life locked in isolation, hindered from loving, touching, or communicating in any way with anyone, including my mother, who was only two years old, and her oldest sister, Barbara, barely four years old at the time.

Grandmother Juanita was a tall, long-limbed, full-of-energy lover of words. Her penmanship spoke with eloquence. Her love of words and wisdom was so strong, it still breathes through me today. She was a woman of God. I have read her letters, all of which read as prayers, as she feared the unknown for her young daughters, who would be left to face the South and this world without her. Nevertheless, God always has a ram in the bush. God's perfect selection was the only grandmother I have ever known.

Even today, thinking about Grandmother Carrie Elizabeth Agnew causes me to tear up.

Grandmother Carrie, or Grandmamma (as in our family culture), cared for my mother and her older sister for almost ten years before having children of her own. God blessed her with three more daughters (Carrie Diana, Debra Denise, and Jane Marie) and one son (John Willie Jr.). As a grandmother, she was my anchor. The place we all ran to in times of need, joy, and suffering. When she first saw Michela, she took her in her arms, kissed her forehead, and said "simply an angel." I agree, Grandmamma, I agree.

After Grandmamma passed over, it became my oldest aunt's destiny to fill her enormous shoes. Just as she observed Grandmamma do, Aunt Bobbie Tubbs and her husband, Uncle Bobbie Tubbs (same first names, too cute right?), held together our entire family unit, helping us to rebuild ourselves as we learned to live without the presence of our big momma, Carrie Elizabeth.

I am standing here as a survivor only because of the love, support, and mentorship I received from so many women God strategically positioned in my life. Teachers like my high school home economics teacher, Mrs. Juarnell Crumbie. Mrs. Crumbie was an old schoolhouse firecracker who would accept nothing but success from her students. Mrs. Crumbie recently passed over to be with God. It is with great personal thanksgiving and professional gratitude I acknowledge a life "well done." She was like a mother, in your face and determined for you to only do your best. Operating below your potential was not acceptable. Connie and Jon, your mother will never be gone. Her legacy and teaching style have roots in us all.

Finally, my "Blessed" mother, Mrs. Robbie Jean Agnew Saulsberry, who married my father, Arthur Lewis Saulsberry Jr., while still a senior in high school. We lived in Nashville near my mother's family until I was in second grade. Then, we moved away from all my mother loved and knew to my father's hometown. My mother is one of a kind. A pearl God set apart just for me. After Michela passed over, our relationship became one of my most challenging to maintain. Maybe because this is how her path began. The sorrowful prayers of a mother unable to touch or comfort her child. Just as her mother, Juanita, was unable to comfort or protect her daughters due to the constraints of quarantine, my mother's geographical location prevented her from comforting me. My mother not only had to deal with her own grief over the loss of her first grandchild, she had to silently watch in anguish as her only daughter's life was spinning out of control. I'm sorry I could not feel you when Michela passed over. I know you were always there. Nevertheless, we made it.

Well done, Momma.
I love you so much.
You are so beautiful, smart, and courageous.
Thank you for modeling grace, forgiveness, and peace before me.
Thank you for always being my biggest supporter.
Most of all, Hallelujah to the Lamb, you brought me to God.

Standing on the promises of God and the shoulders of a long legacy of strong African American Women.

Love jac/duck

Introduction

Have you ever wanted with all your heart to reach out to a grieving person, but were stopped dead in your tracks by feelings of doubt and uncertainty? What do I say? What if I make them think about the situation? What if they don't want to talk? These types of questions can go on and on. The stress and anxiety of desperately wanting to comfort someone you love or know can cause extreme pain, tension, grief, and depression for those forced to patiently watch from the sidelines. The pages in this book will help to quiet those voices. Every word has been tried and tested over countless hours of intimate conversations with our Mighty Comforter, offering us valuable glimpses into the weight associated with the pain and trauma of loss.

This is my journey of success. My declaration to the world. I live and will praise God forevermore. I no longer silently hate God or quietly resent His seemingly inattentive absenteeism during my time of pain. Yes, this book goes there. It will help you to see more clearly the overwhelming evidence of how much God truly cares for His children. This book takes a deep look into the strategic care God provides for all His children. It provides encouragement and guidance to someone who feels they have been called to assist someone to and through their grief journey, or to someone who may be searching for ways to help their current relationship with someone who might be silently struggling in hopeless despair. The four principles provided in this book will help you to love yourself and be fully equipped to comfort your grieving loved one.

CALLED TO SERVICE

Michela Brittany Phelps was born on August 30, 1991. It was one of the most magnificent days of my life, because it took only one glance at her for me to receive and accept the call of motherhood over my life. She was planned for and wanted by both sides of the family. I was designed to be her mother. My husband Courtney and I believed nothing could get to either of our daughters without first coming through us. On June 7, 2003, however, this foolish, temporary truth would be tested and forcibly changed as Michela, at the age of eleven—our first born and the first grandchild on both sides of our family—passed over to our Heavenly Father. Although many will debate whether the transformation to being with God occurs instantaneously or not, for Courtney, our family, our friends, and me, it only meant life without Michela's precious smile.

There was no warning before we were thrust directly into our nightmare. Everything had been going according to my plans. Our family was complete and we were happy.

Sharing the Weight of Grief

Michela Brittany Phelps, six months old

June 7 started just like every Saturday did at that time. I got up early and worked out before work. I had recently transferred to part-time at my job at American Airlines to allow me to complete the first six months of physical therapy school, but even so, my weekend schedule was full to the max. That Saturday was beautiful. I had promised Michela we would all go swim at one of our city aquatic centers. This promise allowed me to give Michela the one thing she loved the most, time in the water—as well as giving me five or six hours of uninterrupted study time. I believe this is why it was so hard and took so long for me to forgive myself. I had corrupted this day with my own selfish need to have uninterrupted study time. The day was less about rewarding Michela and more about taking the kids somewhere they would like so they would not bother me.

Whenever we made plans like this, Michela would count down the hours until I would pull into the driveway after work. As usual, I was running a little late, and Michela began calling around to make sure our plans would not change. I remember my mother calling and explaining to me how important it was to keep my word to Michela. My mother and I have spoken extensively about her call with Michela that morning because it was the last time she spoke to her first grandchild. The conversation was perfect. Michela spoke to my mother about wanting to go swimming but not wanting to have to make lunches or prepare the cooler for the day. My mother suggested that she not just sit there and wait for me to get everything ready. She encouraged Michela to start loading the beach bag and coolers. This conversation happened before noon, and when I arrived home shortly after 2 p.m., Michela was standing in the door with this huge smile on her face. After years of conversation with my mother about this day, I have come to understand Michela was smiling because she had helped me. She was the best helper in the world, always reading my mind. It was like she would study me and then just know what I needed without me saying a word. I opened the door and everything was ready. The only thing I needed to do was to change into my swimsuit and load the kids into my Pontiac Vibe (another blessing Michela helped choose for me).

After asking the last routine question we always asked before leaving—Michela, do you have your inhaler? (check)—we all loaded into the car and headed to the aquatics center. The center was approximately a mile and a half from the duplex we were renting. As always after we arrived, everyone helped to set up our station and received the rules before running to the wave pool. We would always start out drifting around the center in the wave pool, mostly because this gave me the opportunity to check out any rough-looking people and warn the older kids to be on the watch for any suspicious encounters.

After going around the wave pool once, Michela walked over to our newly constructed station and sat down. I noticed she was breathing fast, but she didn't want me to pull the plug on the day. She assured me she just needed to rest a minute. We had been here thousands of times; between asthma camp and swim meets we had become accustomed to pressing through and conquering these minor attacks with ease. My attention must have faded back to studying, because the next memory I have is Michela waving at me from the top of the slide. I can remember telling myself, "If she climbed those stairs? She's fine," and going back to studying with Monica. Monica and I had been friends since we were both freshmen at Tarrant County College (a.k.a. Tarrant County Jr. College/currently TCCD). We were the first recipients to be awarded scholarships under the NIH research grant for undergraduate minorities between TCJC and Texas Woman's University in Denton, Texas. Monica and I were both nontraditional students with families and full-time jobs. Therefore, most of our time was spent together. That Saturday was no different. I can remember us both breathing a sigh of relief once we saw Michela's big smile as she came down the slide. A short time later, Michela came to me and said something she had never before said to me at a water event: "Mommy, I am ready to go home." I looked at her and immediately knew we needed more than an inhaler.

Monica and the other kids stayed at the center while Michela and I went home to give her a treatment on her nebulizer. Michela's nebulizer was part of her treatment plan and vital to her preventive care. The medication for the nebulizer, albuterol, comes in a box with four foil pouches. Each pouch contains five 3 mL vials. Michela's preventive plan required two vials. When we got home, our first stop was to the nebulizer bag. I opened the bag and took out the nebulizer and saline, then reached for one of the foil pouches. There were none. I went to her swim bag. Empty. I checked the bathroom, her school backpack, and sleepover bags. Nothing. I went to the refrigerator to retrieve one of the many boxes we usually have for backup. None. There was no albuterol in the house. I immediately got angry at Michela and told her to get in the car. We went to the pharmacy and made it all the way back home before realizing they had given me the wrong medication.

By that time, Michela was wheezing badly and asked if she could stay home and wait for me in bed. I allowed her to stay and returned back to the pharmacy. I was still very upset at Michela for not telling me she had opened the last box of albuterol, but tried to be less angry because she was starting to cry, and crying makes breathing even more difficult. I remember apologizing and telling her it was just super important she take her medicine seriously and not ever let it get low. The most important thing was keeping her out of the ER. When her breathing became too labored, off to Cook Children's Medical Center we would go. Sometimes it would be a brief visit, but sometimes this would mean a stay at the hospital. Annually, she would spend at least ten to fifteen days in Cook Children's Intensive Care Unit receiving intravenous steroids. One of my biggest concerns while attending physical therapy school was to keep Michela healthy.

Looking back, I'm extremely critical of my behavior throughout the course of that day. Yes, I was very distracted. However, it was my responsibility, not that of an eleven-year-old, to make sure the albuterol was fully stocked. At the time, I was just frustrated my study time was being derailed by having to run back and forth to the pharmacy. By the time I returned home with the correct medication and got Michela on her nebulizer, Courtney was pulling into the drive. I explained to him that either he or Michela had used the last vial without telling me and that she was on the machine. Once she finished her treatment, I asked if she was ready to return to the aquatics center—and to my surprise, she said, "No ma'am, I am going to stay home with Daddy." This never happened. But even though it gave me pause, I still left her there with my husband and two of her uncles, my oldest brother and Courtney's oldest brother. My plan was to pick up the other kids and come directly home.

I remember getting there and finding Monica already had our station and kids packed. I don't remember any of the usual complaints from the younger kids about staying longer or anything. What I do remember is being at the stoplight by my house and having Courtney blowing my phone up. I was so close to home, I just decided not to answer. When I pulled into the drive, I saw my brother-in-law, Lamont, on the phone, my brother, Lewis, on the ground holding his head, and Courtney and Michela nowhere to be found. Lewis and Lamont never looked at me. Monica and I ran into the house, and there was Michela on the floor. We immediately began CPR. It seemed like hours before the fire department and EMT arrived. I can remember trying to breathe air into her body and getting upset because all attempts to give her air turned into bubbles and would not pass the bronchial block.

Once the EMT arrived, they attempted to get a pulse but could not. They continued CPR—at least in front of us. But this led to another huge regret for me: why did we allow them to take her in the ambulance without a parent? Why did I not demand to ride in the ambulance with my daughter, to not just leave her again? Courtney and I drove behind the ambulance, praying for God to intervene and save us. I knew God would never take Michela from me. I knew just enough scriptures to get myself all worked up.

We arrived at Arlington Memorial Hospital and they immediately took us to a separate area to wait. A young doctor came in and told me that my baby had expired. What? I asked, "Does expired mean–" and everything went blank from that point. I can remember Courtney explaining that she was fine, that she had told him she felt better and was thirsty. He continued trying to explain to this ER doctor how she was fine, and how he went to get her water and bring it back to her. He had felt like something was wrong and returned just as Michela said "Daddy" and reached for him. According to Courtney, it was that fast, and she did not struggle.

I have come to believe, over the years, Courtney and our brothers will never tell me exactly what they experienced. The bottom line is my daughter passed over to be with the Lord on June 7 at 5:25 p.m. after having a fatal low bronchial spasm. God decided my husband and our older brothers would be there, but not me or the other kids. Of course, I begged and pleaded with Courtney for step-by-step reenactments of the day. My medical background just would not allow me to leave it alone. Even after Michela's doctor and nurse went over the autopsy with me and assured me it was instant, I still felt like everyone was lying to me. Because of my research background, it takes evidence "data" to persuade me of anything. Nevertheless, God knows exactly who to send in our times of need. I remember receiving this unexpected call from one of the pulmonary nurses from Cook's Children. As I listened, she explained exactly how I was feeling. She also explained how sudden her child's attack occurred, which began to help me accept Courtney's version of events.

I do not think I will ever completely surrender this need to know all the details. Nevertheless, I have learned to be thankful. I am thankful God saw fit to spare my heart. Even though I have some idea of how it happened, I am sure it is nothing compared to Courtney's nightmare. I understand watching Michela's soul leave her body might have been too much for me mentally. This journey teaches how to seek thankfulness from the most unlikely places. Like being able to recover your child's remains to bury or lay to rest. Yes, I was thrust into fully grasping this during our family's group counseling meetings at the WARM Place as we listened to other families' never-ending questions surrounding not being able to bury their children due to fires, drownings, or abductions. I quickly learned how to be thankful even when my heart was breaking. This was probably one of my first lessons. Grief picks you up and places you inside of a bubble. At first glance, it seems to be very selfish and self-serving. However, more than a bubble of selfishness, it is a bubble of survival: God's perfect protection. You can trust that no matter how tragic your loved one's story may be, God is there. God has written the perfect story. He has placed and will continue to place each person in the perfect position to complete His will.

Now, over eighteen years later, I understand that June 7 was my initial call into service. And now, just as I was, you have been called for an act of service. The huge difference or game changer is the Holy Spirit, who is here to assist you. Even though there will be much required. There is great news for those of us who trust the leading of the Holy Spirit: service does not mean work. It means sacrificially placing the will of the Father before your own thoughts and ways. Our Heavenly Father who is omnipotent and omnipresent does not need you to come and lean to your own understandings, your own thoughts and ways. Our thoughts and ways will lead us straight toward attempting to work things out for ourselves (i.e. works of the flesh). Although this type of help can be heartfelt, and even biblically sound sometimes, it is not the most effective means of reasonable servitude. Works of the flesh simply will not cut it on grief journeys, as works of the flesh are usually temporary and self-motivated in nature. Nevertheless, as we have found ourselves here during this season, as we embark on a journey toward the Father's unrevealed truth, we will practice trusting and serving based on the infallible Word of God. This concept, trusting God, will be used often throughout the book. Yes, there are other ways to seek help, and I have used many of them with good results. However, nothing works better for God's children than the infallible Word of God.

From this point forward, as you read and apply the truths within this book, your posture must always be bold and confident, acknowledging Jesus as Lord of all things. This boldness will come, grow, and manifest its true self through the leading and guiding of the Holy Spirit. "For those who are led by the Spirit of God are the children of God" (Romans 8:14, NIV). As we begin by acknowledging this, the Father will help us to lean not to our own understanding, but rather to invite, allow, and accept the guidance of the Holy Spirit as we diligently commit to interceding on the behalf of those in need.

Now that we have briefly visited the leading author, the Holy Spirit, and acknowledged He is speaking to God's children in the pages of this book, we can outline four key principles every believer who desires to intercede on the behalf of another should be aware of prior to starting this wonderful sacrificing journey.

Principle 1: The work belongs to God

Just as Simon of Cyrene assisted Jesus with carrying the cross, our position as supporters is to assist our loved ones on their journeys. These are journeys that will lead them to a deeper understanding of God's expected end for their own personal lives. This means, as a supporter, you must place and keep yourself in the background as much as possible. This does not mean posting notes all over your grieving loved one's home and workspace, or forcing them to pray out loud in the Spirit, just because these things work for you. Although both of these tasks are beneficial, it is through the leading of the Holy Spirit in which we speak and walk. As you position yourself in the background, await on His call to speak or not speak, walk or not walk, for "If we live in the Spirit, let us also walk in the Spirit" (Galatians 5:25, KJV). I have often caught myself saying things such as, "Let me quickly pray for you," or "The only thing we can do is pray." In the pages of this book, intercessory prayer is our first response, because it has never failed and will never lead us astray. It is through prayer and supplication those supporting my initial journey to and through grief waited, with great expectation, for God's perfect plan to begin to sprout, bringing itself into full fruition. Momma, I am here now!

One of the great privileges granted to all believers is the power of prayer. Prayers allow us to intercede on someone's behalf without even being in close proximity. I am reminded of the faithful centurion whose servant was sick with palsy at home (Please reference Matthew 8:5–13). This man was convinced, without any reservation, Jesus had so much authority, He could just speak a word, and his sick servant would be healed. You will need to hold this same kind of unshakable faith in your prayers.

As you become more and more silent, your grieving loved one will become more and more reliant on God. I would love to tell you the road of being a committed supporter will be easy, fun, and always understood. But in your own thoughts and ways, trying to do things based on your own emotions and perspectives, it will not be easy or light. When God calls us to service, He is calling us to be sacrificial as we find Him in all things great and small. Most people would classify me as a "call it as I see it" kind of girl. Therefore, allow me to be painfully honest: If I had been Simon of Cyrene on that crucifixion Friday, I am not sure my answer would have been "yes."

Although we are not given many facts about Jesus' supporter, scripture does record Simon of Cyrene's call and his obedient reply. We also know Simon was a worshipper of the God of the Jews. This most likely meant he was a dispersed Jewish man who had returned for the Passover celebration. Scriptures detail Simon's day by indicating he was accompanied by his two sons in obedience to the law when he was ordered by Roman soldiers to assist in Jesus' crucifixion. I would have been very apprehensive to bring this type of attention and danger to my family. Nevertheless, we can still hold to several truths here: First, God chose, called, and protected Simon of Cyrene and his entire family. Next, he was strategically positioned in God's plan to save all humanity. Therefore, if God has called you to service, He will lead and protect you, too. Lastly, the service was uniquely prescribed for Simon to assist Jesus. He was not walking beside Jesus, encouraging Him to push past the pain. No, I am sure Simon of Cyrene's breath was taken away to see Jesus in His weakened state, battered and bruised from His flogging and brutal disfigurement. It is this type of silent posture you must prayerfully reach and maintain, as you will undoubtedly feel unequipped at times to manage such a heavy load. God tells us to try Him and see if He will not pour a blessing into you that you will not be able to contain (Malachi 3:10b). It is my belief your supplications and fervent prayers will shower down to those who are mourning, the blessed. Therefore, we must remain in a posture of continual prayer and supplication to our Lord.

Principle 2: Silence is more than okay, it is vital

Sometimes the most unintentional words can be received in the most unexpected ways. I can remember, especially during the early months of my journey through grief, being thrown completely off balance by words that would have been better kept silent. They were words loving, well-meaning believers would say in truth, but those words were not loving toward my current heart situation. We need to remember the adversary is there, waiting to use any and all opportunities to isolate those who grieve from the watchful, caring arms of their loved ones. By the time this book is published, it will be 2021. In June our family would have made it to and through our journey without Michela for eighteen years. Now, I can more clearly understand "what they meant to say" and the rest was just unwise fleshly attempts to help.

PRINCIPLE 3: THE HOLY SPIRIT IS THE MASTER TEACHER

Although **Principles 1 and 2** are important, we cannot make it through this grief journey successfully and wholly unless we learn to lean not to our own understanding of the situation we find ourselves in. During the Last Supper, Jesus proclaimed "One greater than I will come." Then, on the day of Pentecost, the Holy Spirit became available to all (Acts 2:1–41). This means once we become believers, our lifelong task is "becoming." Which means desiring to become more and more reliant on God through the leading of the Holy Spirit. The main problem when it comes to grief and the Holy Spirit is quietness. The voice of the Holy Spirit is gentle, comforting, and very courteous—and requires active intentional listening.

Jesus has already done the work; the Holy Spirit is there to gently guide us to God's expected and perfect seasons within our journeys. We have a gentle, attentive master teacher dwelling inside of us all. Your grieving loved one has a gentle and attentive master teacher dwelling inside of him or her, too. Just as we submit to the initial workings of the Holy Spirit's amazing power in the repentant heart of a new believer, we must believe our intercessory prayers combined with the same powerful workings of the Holy Spirit are sufficient to arrest and overcome any and all circumstances.

The prophet Ezekiel watched dry skeletons stand up, grow new flesh, and breathe again (Ezekiel 37:1–14). Just as I have risen and can joyfully breathe again, your grieving loved one will stand up and breathe again, too. God has not and will not leave nor forsake any of His children, especially during times of despair. We must position ourselves in confidence and boldness, with a pure-hearted commitment to intercede, and not intervene, as we fully come to trust God's truth without wavering. As the supporter, just like Simon, you will ever so gently help to bear the load of walking this journey alone. Not only will your grieving loved one experience an everlasting change, you will also be renewed. As you quietly observe, listen, and pray, you too will be forever changed as you position yourself to surrender more and more to the guidance of the Holy Spirit.

What makes the Holy Spirit so powerful? First, He is God. This means He is omnipotent and omnipresent, with all the characteristics we attribute to the Father and the Son, as the Trinity. In the beginning, the Spirit of God moved across the face of the waters, and God said, "Let there be light." This is the same Holy Spirit Jesus speaks of in John 14:16 (KJV), saying "and I will pray the Father, and He shall give you another Comforter, that He may abide with you for ever." Jesus continues to proclaim the truth and power of the Holy Spirit who "dwelleth with you, and shall be in you" (John 14:17c, KJV). If you apply this key truth to your support of your loved one, it will come to pass. It is Jesus who proclaims our victory in Him through His good and perfect gifts which flow from above (James 1:17).

Second, He dwells among us. The very location of the Holy Spirit is supernaturally perfect, as previously witnessed by Jesus' own words, that He dwells with you and shall be in you. This means the Holy Spirit is housed exactly where the grieving condition is. Grief is, at its simplest and most complex, a condition of the heart. How great is the Father to place His comfort for the brokenhearted through the rich red, healing blood of Jesus right in the middle of the action! This is the reason it is so important to allow the Holy Spirit to deal with the affairs of the heart.

It might help to think of this in terms of a surgical procedure. If a physician decided to operate on you without first taking blood work or X-rays, you would jump off the table and flee. This is exactly what we do when we intervene instead of interceding through the guidance of the Holy Spirit. The Holy Spirit's words, given in obedience to His guidance, will never harm or fail, which makes them especially helpful for the peculiar and particular needs of the broken. God has been preparing us to be redeemed since the fall of man. Therefore, it is only reasonable to believe His Word when it proclaims He will not leave us or forsake us during our times of trouble (Deuteronomy 31:6). You can trust God's truth and lean on it in times of uncertainty, weakness, or frustration—all of which are common during journeys of grief. Nevertheless, we will be learning, practicing, and mastering the art of taking those thoughts and emotions captive, making them obedient to Christ (2 Corinthians 10:5). As we move through the pages of this book, pray for more and more discernment. Although the Holy Spirit has given me the power to share my journey, all of God's children have an inherited right to seek and find their own way. The power of the Holy Spirit which dwells inside of you is also available for your grieving loved one. We learn and then implement what we have learned as we master interceding and not intervening for those who are mourning.

Principle 4: The journey belongs to your grieving loved one

I am in a state of continually learning this key principle. Our family received an overflow of support and help during our journey through grief. Of course, the most beneficial came from those who were led to us by the Holy Spirit. Courtney and I were not mentally or physically strong enough to do anything but exist during the first few years of life without Michela. Nevertheless, like a good parent, God sent many goodly Simons our way. Some were believers. Some were not. All, however, provided different types of support, love, and comfort throughout our journey. One thing I have learned is to not be overly concerned with the vessel being used. As Jesus informed His disciples, "Do not stop him, for no one who does a miracle in My name can in the next moment say anything bad about Me" (Mark 9:39, NIV). Trust God, and surrender the work of figuring things out, such as the motivations of others and their opinions concerning your motives, to God. Just keep on praying. The work, the surrendering, the moving to and through the phases and stages of grief—all belong to God and to the person who has come to a place of need. We all have to bring our questions, doubts, hurts, pains, and sorrows to the cross. As with Jesus and Simon of Cyrene, God will send help—but it is important to intercede, not intervene. The Father wants and requires a personal relationship with all His children. It is this same Father who does not need our help, yet allows and grants us the privilege to guide our loved ones' broken and bruised hearts to Him.

If there was one thing that sustained Courtney's and my marriage past the gruesome statistics of divorce after the passing of a child, it was, and continues to be, our ability to surrender the work of comforting each other to God. At times, Courtney would be curled up, crying like a baby over what I can only imagine as a parent's worst nightmare: to hold your firstborn daughter in your arms as she passes from the physical to the spiritual. It seemed I could do nothing to ease his pain. He held on to the pain because as my king, lover, and soulmate he wanted (and still wants) to spare me from having to know all the details of Michela's last physical moments. Therefore, we quickly mastered the art of allowing the other person to grieve.

Our family had a code—"Michela Day." This meant, "Please excuse me, and leave me alone." There were times in which I was the griever, lying on the bathroom floor screaming at the top of my lungs, or stuck in my car at the grocery store, unable to breathe. There were times when I was the supporter, cleaning up a mess from the floor after one of Courtney's many implosions. As the supporter, it is important to remain silent as you prayerfully intercede. It is important to be on the peripheral, yet respectfully close as you observe your grieving loved one's journey. You cannot truly provide accurate assistance from the sidelines. We allow the Holy Spirit to have His perfect way as we feed, clothe, and care for the brokenhearted. You are the hands and feet of God, but you must allow room for the Holy Spirit in His own timing to remove, rebuild, restore, and nurture into development everything your grieving loved one needs. You are the observer, the one called out from the crowd to come along beside your grieving loved one. You are intimate enough to know exactly how to pray as you stand ready to assist as led by the Holy Spirit.

It was so strange to me at first when the Holy Spirit would show Himself strong in my situations. I have now come to expect and welcome with great anticipation God's movement through the Holy Spirit. Now, looking back, I understand more. I can see that this was always the Father's perfected plan, a plan that was impossible for me to see or comprehend through my tear-soaked eyes.

Remember, although **Principle 4** aligns with biblical truth, we can still trust God's desire for us to "grope for Him and find Him, though He is not far from each one of us" (Acts 17:27b, NKJV). As vigilant and intimately committed seekers of the truth, we should never be fearful when led by the Spirit to reach out for help. As a committed supporter, you might be required to do difficult things when necessary. This might mean seeking confidential, professional advice or help. This is part of what you are accepting: being a committed and observant interceder with a heart of discernment toward the will of God. As a supporter of the grieving process, it is important to observe with the commitment to seek God's assistance and the confidence to know when it might be time to call for outside help.

Please understand, if you feel at any time that you or your grieving loved one have moved beyond your abilities, you should reach out for assistance—it is never wrong to seek help, and 911 is always available. Although your commitment and dedication is to walk with the griever spiritually, we are blessed to be in a season of many resources. Sometimes it will take more—and that is okay. Your assistance cannot comfort, pray away, or adequately manage the signs and symptoms of complicated grief. Complicated grief has been referred to as "traumatic grief," "complicated grief disorder," and "prolonged grief" (Iglewicz et al. 2020), and it is distinctly different from depression "accounted for by bereavement," as mentioned in the *Diagnostic and Statistical Manual of Mental Disorders, Fourth Edition (DSM-IV)*. Complicated grief is included in the *DSM-5* under the name "persistent complex bereavement disorder" (Malgaroli et al. 2018). As supporters of grieving loved ones, we must be watchful for the signs and symptoms associated with complicated grief and be ready to reach out to professionals with the background and credentials to assist. Signs and symptoms of complicated grief may include, but are not limited to:

- Focus on little else but your loved one's death
- Intense sorrow, pain, and rumination over the loss of your loved one
- Intense and persistent longing or pining for the deceased
- Numbness or detachment
- Problems accepting the death
- Bitterness about your loss
- Feeling life holds no meaning or purpose
- Lack of trust in others
- Inability to enjoy life or think back on positive experiences with your loved one.

Research suggests, of the population experiencing bereavement, complicated grief affects between 9 percent and 20 percent (Iglewicz et al. 2020), with variations based upon social, cultural, and clinical background as well as age. Complicated grief strongly affects the wellbeing of the bereaved (Scott et al. 2020), and it is associated with sleep disturbances (Hardison et al. 2005), depression and a higher risk of suicide (Tal et al. 2017), abuse of alcohol (Hardison et al. 2005), and poor health (Albuquerque et al. 2016). In addition, psychosocial risks such as a loss, unexpected death, or suicide (Nielson et al. 2017; Becker et al. 2014); lack of social support; and/or inability to adapt to the resulting changes have also been indentified as key factors (Robinson et al., 2006; Ott, 2003). However, the ultimate cause of complicated grief is not well established. If the road, situation, or hurdle you are facing reveals itself as a sign or symptom of complicated grief, please seek immediate professional assistance.

Please understand the previous information has been researched and peer reviewed based on the standards of national and international scholarly databases. These are valid and reliable secular research-based theories, which flow from and align with the infallible Word of God. My science and research background loves data. Nevertheless, data must also bow down to the authority of King Jesus. It was peer-supported statistical data that predicted my marriage would fail after the death of Michela (Albuquerque et al. 2016; Finnäs et al. 2018; Malgaroli et al. 2018). Data shows grieving parents not only deal with sorrow following the loss of a child, they also face stressors, such as restructured family roles or grieving siblings, which can have implications for marital stability and increase the risk of divorce (Finnäs et al. 2018). Yet we are here, still standing and more in love than before we started this journey. Blessed to have celebrated our thirty-third wedding anniversary on January 4, 2021. God's love flourishes and stands tall against all things, including secular data and statistics.

Do not allow any of this to make you afraid or reluctant to commit. You can still use every principle within the pages of this book to travel along beside your grieving loved one, whether they have decided to utilize a professional or are choosing to walk this journey using a multitude of helpful resources. This book has been purposefully designed as one of those gentle, assistive resources. You can take or leave as much as you need. All healing and acceptance flows from our shared experiences and wisdom as believers in Christ Jesus. His blood gives us the power to access, stand on, and apply these experiences as truth. Your wisdom will only assist whatever journey the griever ultimately decides to take.

We have now covered our cornerstone principles, and we are ready to start this wonderful journey toward a deeper and fuller understanding of the Father's plan for your life during this season. As you proceed through these pages, my desire is to keep it simple, relevant, and beneficial. In order to do this, you will need to align my words with scripture, trust God's Word as truth regardless of the messenger, and allow the Holy Spirit and the finished works of Jesus to minister to you as you read each page. Always align my words to the infallible Word of God. If it does not align to the Word of God for you, no worries. Realign, remove, or leave it on the table.

As hard as it might be to hear, some things are simply situational; only the Word of God is infallible. You don't have to write me or email me if something in this book does not fit you. Yes, I would love for you to be able to receive and digest every word. What good chef wouldn't? But you are setting a new table, one unique to you and your grieving loved one. Therefore, it's okay to take as much or as little as you desire. Pick it up or set it down and come back for leftovers. It's your table, and it is completely okay, because my trust is in the Father. The Father gave me this book, and I lean confidently on Him. He will use it as He sees fit. Therefore, just as I have learned, you must also not lean to your own understanding, but rather trust what the Father has given us in His infallible Word. You must be committed to be ready, which simply means to stay in the Word of God, never ceasing to remember to pray and to acknowledge the Father in all His ways. Those things declared by His precious blood are available and ready to lead you to and through your journey, just the same as I was led. I can stand firm on God's character, "for there is no respect of persons with God" (Romans

2:11, KJV). This means that, as healing is available for me, healing is available to all those who love the Lord and who call on Him.

The most important takeaway within this conversation is "you can trust God." If doubt comes, please remember my testimony of almost eighteen years. God has a strategic plan for all His children. As you read this book, He is offering you tangible evidence in your hands. He is real. I am still here. I am full of joy. I can receive and give love. Most importantly, my faith in and love for the Father is deeper and stronger than ever before. This is why you can trust what you are receiving throughout the pages of this book: every word typed and delivered to you has been tried, tested, and given the Father's anointed seal of approval. My life has been given and purposed to honor the Father. If you follow these simple steps, you will not only be sharing the load for a grieving, broken-hearted person, you will also be forever changed. It is impossible for me to explain how caring for others more than yourself comes back to the giver so fully. Scripture supports this through the words of our Father and the life of Jesus Christ, our Savior: "A new commandment I give to you, that you love one another, even as I have loved you, that you also love one another" (John 13:34, NASB). You are guaranteed a great heavenly return on your investment.

Deeper Look at Principle 1: The Work Belongs to God

The work belongs to God. This principle must be your cornerstone. It is vital for your own health and peace of mind for you to be in a constant state of remembering to implement this truth throughout your walk of intercession. In order to surrender the work, we must trust that the Father is equipped to handle, direct, and lead us out of whatever situation we find ourselves. We must believe God has a master plan and be grateful He is blessing us to help. We are not the master plan; rather, we are contributors to the perfect will of the Father. Whenever you become frustrated or overwhelmed, ask yourself, "Am I trusting God, or rushing God?" We serve an almighty God who will not harm us, even if we are innocently reaching out of childlike ignorance or foolish resistance.

As the support of someone who is grieving, you must be able to surrender your thoughts and ways to the Father's infallible thoughts and ways. You must be able to recognize when you might be leaning to your own thoughts and ways, especially when dealing with the multifaceted affairs associated with matters of the heart, such as grief. When dealing with grief, lines can and will become very blurred. I can remember the overwhelming fear I had for Erica, who was only five years old when Michela passed over. The fear she would follow in her sister's footsteps and be overtaken by asthma before the age of twelve paralyzed me for years. I thought she would never be a whole, healthy adult. How could she, when I am so broken? But Erica turned twenty-three years old on December 28, 2020. She is strong, healthy, and fully cured from asthma. She has not had a need for albuterol or steroids in over two years. The only sad part of this past reflection is the days, nights, and weeks in which I suffered needlessly because of not trusting God. The amount of power I gave the enemy, the years of emotional roller coasters, the hijacking of my peace, joy, and destiny—all because, through the grief, I could not release the one thing I thought I still controlled: my own thoughts and ways.

Therefore, getting **Principle 1** down in your soul is vital for this journey, not only for the griever, but for you the supporter as well. God the Father cares for *your* body, mind, and soul, too. He desires to take good care of all His investments. You, my friend, have been selected, called out of the crowd just as Simon was, into one of God's most precious promises to those who mourn: "Blessed are those who mourn, for they shall be comforted" (Matthew 5:4, NASB). You have been selected in this season to comfort.

I unknowingly wasted precious time feeling frustrated, worrying, and working to prevent Erica from being a victim to asthma like Michela, when all I needed to do was to allow God's perfect will to be done. God's perfect will can be done here in your situation, too. I cannot promise you will not be visited by feelings of fear, doubt, or frustration as you intercede on your loved one's behalf. I can tell you, choosing to cast that fear, doubt, or frustration on God will eventually produce results you can testify to. I will prayerfully assume, because you are still reading this book, you believe that help, guidance, and victory are possible. And they are! As you open yourself more and more to possibilities such as beauty for ashes, oil of joy for mourning, and a garment of praise for a spirit of heaviness (Isaiah 61:3, KJV), the enemy will undoubtedly come up against you. You cannot be a babe on watered-down milk and intercede here. Rather, you must be mature, for this book is for those ready for solid food (Hebrews 5:12–14). You must become an A plus student at being a goodly child of the Most High God. We become masters at this by acknowledging and openly confessing this in all our thoughts (the way we think) and ways (the way we walk), and in the conversations we have with ourselves and others (the way we talk). As you model this quietly before the griever, you will indeed create space for the griever to eventually follow suit. It is the repetitive implementation of these types of simple strategies over time which will gently lead your grieving loved one toward surrendering those exhausting, temporary, and permissible thoughts and emotions to God.

During my journey through grief, my questions would keep me up at night and distract me throughout my day. I would ponder over how scriptures like Psalm 37:4 (ESV) could state, "Delight yourself in the Lord, and He will give you the desires of your heart." Delight myself? He will give me the desires of my heart, *really*? Was God so unfamiliar with me, His child, that He thinks this was my desire? My body was attempting to bring me into balance physically, but my mind was totally derailed. You must remember, these are the feelings of uncertainty that believers ponder over during different times of their journey when their minds and hearts are being consumed by grief. My entire world had been turned upside down. When trauma occurs suddenly, it can leave those affected unhinged. If the traumatic event is new or has never been experienced, it can be very difficult to rationalize new emotions. My emotions would flood in and out like tsunami waves. Most days this made it very difficult and exhausting to share with others, mainly because my emotions seemed to be randomly uncontrollable. Everything reminded me of what I had lost. Every aspect of my life was touched: my eating, sleeping, working, and resting were all disjointed. I was not able to even hold Erica and feel her love, or embrace my husband romantically, because any joy was accompanied by extreme guilt and sorrow.

During some parts of your grieving loved one's journey, some seasons may seem to extend to every aspect of the griever's existence. It is during these seasons when the Father's perfect will is being done—trust the truth and lean hard on God. You must be confident and bold in the Word of God which proclaims that your grieving loved one will live and not die. "I shall not die, but live, and declare the works of the Lord" (Psalm 118:17, KJV). Trust the truth; as Job proclaims, "Though He slay me, yet will I trust in Him: but I will maintain mine own ways before Him" (Job 13:15, KJV). Please be aware, however, this is not information you should share with the griever, as it will only hurt them in their time of grief. Rather, it is something the griever needs to come to understand on their own. Remember, it is their journey, so you need to act according to their timing and not yours. Every word you speak must be filtered through the infallible Word of God for each moment and specific situation. God will position you perfectly from the periphery to patiently observe. This will give you room to quietly and prayerfully discern the situation before taking action or speaking. Some truths can be just too much and too soon for your grieving loved one's heart, mind, and soul to receive at a given part of their journey.

A perfect example of this comes from when my husband rededicated his life to Christ and was baptized shortly after our daughter's home-going celebration. Courtney and I were raised in the same church, and it was customary for children to give their lives to Christ and be baptized at age twelve. My husband decided to join with a number of his friends who were also turning twelve to be baptized. It was a group event they were all committing to do together. When Courtney's grandmother found out the particulars concerning Courtney's reasoning or lack thereof, she refused to allow him to participate in the outward expression of his faith at that time. She wanted him to accept Christ only when he understood the magnitude of his actions. Whether correct or not, the takeaway is that from twelve to thirty-seven years of age, God was still patiently waiting on Courtney's outward expression of his acceptance of Him. Michela's home-going celebration was on a Friday; the following Sunday, Courtney gave his life to Christ and was baptized shortly thereafter. As a saint, my heart, mind, and soul were on cloud nine. As a wife, I could not have been prouder. As the supporter of a griever, I should have stayed quiet.

A goodly supporter would have been less focused on what I've always wanted, Deacon Courtney Phelps, and remained silent while the Holy Spirit was speaking so clearly and soundly to him. Instead, one day when I was feeling all preachy and overly anointed to share my revelation concerning Courtney's grief, I made a noisy statement, noisy because it was not a word for me to give. Even today, I would do anything to take it back. Yes, it was biblical and it aligned with scripture, but it was the wrong time, and my delivery sucked big time. I stated, "Michela is rejoicing that you were baptized because of her death." The look on Courtney's face was as if I had taken a dagger and thrust it into his heart. I tried to explain, but nothing I said made any difference. My words, even if truth, created a vessel of despair for my husband and continued to torture our relationship for years. For many years, these damaging words would be brought back to his mind whenever we would have disagreements. Fortunately, we were able to make it through those dark times, and Courtney has even come to understand my initial intentions were good.

I share this testimony with you in hopes it will spare you from ever having to see this type of hurt in the eyes of your grieving loved one. The best cure for a noisy truth is remaining prayerfully quiet, allowing the Holy Spirit to give you the words to say in every season of this journey, prayerfully discerning that you will be anxious for nothing, but through prayer and supplication, you will become better and better at making your requests known to God. Then you must trust Him as you wait, anticipating clarity, healing, and peace. We must always be mindful of our ultimate goal to assist, comfort, and support our loved one to a fuller relationship with their only perfect and complete help, which is God. This help comes as the griever moves ever so gracefully toward Job's response. The Hebrew translation makes it very clear: "Behold, he will kill me; I have no hope. Nevertheless, I will maintain my ways before him" (Job 13:15, HNV). Job the griever proclaims his truths, even without hope he will trust in God. Sometimes, those of us who have the closest walk with the Father have the hardest time openly admitting trouble with accepting Job's truth. Can I trust Him? Is this truth for me? As your grieving loved one is finding their way toward a deeper understanding, you must hold fast to their fallen truths. During this time you might feel like a caretaker of forgotten, hidden, and unforeseen promises. Gently remind yourself to lean not to your own understanding and to forgive weakness quickly. I had to forgive myself for making that statement to Courtney. The Father reminded me that His grace is sufficient for me, for His power is made perfect in weakness (2 Corinthians 12:9). So, stay clear of noisy truths and forgive yourself quickly if one shines through.

Today, I can boldly testify with complete confidence, along with Job, "Though He slay me, yet will I have hope in Him." I have grown over the years to learn not to lean to or desire my own understanding, but rather to trust God, especially when it does not feel good or seems to be downright unbearable. As the supporter, it is important for you to model a peaceful surrendering to God before your grieving loved one.

Deeper Look at Principle 2: Silence Is More than Okay, It Is Vital!

Principle 2 is vital. Silence is okay. We must remember to be comfortable with quietness during conversations with someone who is grieving, especially during the initial months of the loss. It is during these early moments of the journey that being silent and allowing the Holy Spirit to guide your thoughts, actions, and tongue are the most useful. You must learn the art of allowing someone to present questions while you silently pray, only interrupting to gently nudge them closer to remaining present. If the griever asks, "How could this happen?" or "Why did God allow this to happen to me?" a gentle way of "keeping them present" would be for you to model breathing. As they talk, sob, or scream, you can model intentional, deep rhythmic breaths from your diaphragm. When you do speak, it should be purposeful and guarded or not at all. Being quiet will provide the space for your grieving loved one to eventually hear the words that are flowing from their heart. It's okay if they repeat the same phrases, no matter how silly, strange, or odd they may seem to you. Allow them to repeat their words over and over again, however long it may take. This process is temporarily needed in order to move your grieving loved one from one stage or phase to another. Each experience, no matter how insignificant it might seem, will usher them closer and closer to God's understanding, rather than their own.

When I have received questions from those who have been called from the crowd to assist in the support of someone's grief journey, most of them are related to the frustration of being unable to assist in a meaningful way. The weight and torment of the first encounters with someone dealing with seemingly overwhelming grief can be unsettling. You might wonder, "What do I say?" or "When is a good time?" Job provides us with a great example. He eloquently makes this fundamental principle clear to his three friends in Job 13:1–16. According to Job's own words, his three friends would have served him better if they had simply followed **Principle 2** and embraced the godliness in being quiet.

In the Bible, Job has questions concerning the motives of his three friends. I am prayerfully assuming by this point of my book your motives are clear: you are here because you have been called, not out of duty or obligation. Once again, works of the flesh won't cut it here. **Principle 2** fundamentally holds to the truth that being silent and praying is vital and should be your first response to all questions during your griever's journey. The primary takeaway for us is spoken so well by Job as he pleads with those attempting to support his grieving process to leave him alone so he could speak with God (Job 13:13). You must hold to the truth and trust not only for yourself but also for your griever that being silent, even during moments of great questioning, will eventually lead to God. There is absolutely nothing your spoken words can do to persuade a broken heart to be better. Only the infallible Word of God, the completed work of our Lord and Savior on the cross, and the guidance of the Holy Spirit can comfort someone through the uncertainty and questions of overwhelming grief. I use the words uncertainty and questions because even if the loss comes after a long battle with a disease or illness, the griever still has not entered, and sometimes has been hindered from entering, into any of the phases or stages of grief. These stages and phases are not fixed, and at times might even seem to be gently or forcibly blended. This means your ability to assess which stage, phase, or combination of stages and phases your loved one is currently experiencing is weak.

I will intentionally overuse the word "weak" throughout this book. It is my prayerful hope that by the end of our journey together, "weak" will bring your soul into an overwhelming closeness to your Heavenly Father's strength as He transforms your crooked thinking to align with His infallible Word. We welcome our weakness, because our awareness of our inability to be stronger than God, or to be "weak," leads us to the best solution for all trials and tribulations, especially those related to the passing over of a loved one. We turn to God's Word, Jesus' work on the cross, and the comfort of the Holy Spirit. Therefore, although we need to know and recognize the stages and phases of grief, we are not controlling which stage your loved one is in, how long they experience it, or whether they will or will not experience a certain stage. Your work is to daily surrender all to God as you prayerfully observe and quietly model peaceful trust in the Father's truths.

For the purpose of providing applicable, bite-sized pieces of help during specific times of trouble typically experienced by those who are grieving, six possible stages or phases will be identified—shock, denial, anger, guilt, sorrow or depression, and acceptance—which will lead to the last and most purposeful stage or phase, of engaging in life anew. Each stage or phase will be defined and you will be provided examples and prayerful solutions to assist in the application and successful implementation of the four key principles. It is the prayerful intention of this book to equip every supporter with the spiritual armor to stand and confidently intercede for one of God's children. Once completed, the book has been designed for easy access with the **Quick Reference Guide**. It has been designed specifically by the Holy Spirit to allow easy access in times of need. As we begin to review each stage or phase, remember grief involves a broken or bruised heart that has lost its hope. Matters of the heart cannot be neatly placed into timeframes or concrete mindsets. Just as our Heavenly Father moves through us, you must discern, receive, and then tailor-make my words and testimony based on the leading of the Holy Spirit and your grieving loved one's needs.

Deeper Look at Principle 3: The Holy Spirit Is the Master Teacher

Principle 3 must be your guide. The Holy Spirit is the master teacher. As you become more and more comfortable with **Principles 1 and 2**, you will surely be more successful at leaning to God's understanding and not your own. There is absolutely no one greater than Jesus is. This same Jesus stated in the second chapter of Acts, "One greater than He would come." **Principle 3** confesses this truth.

As believers or someone considering options available to those who believe, **Principle 3** aligns with our lifelong task of "becoming." This is the ultimate goal of the Holy Spirit, whom we call by name, to help us become more and more aware of God's presence in all situations and circumstances. Remember to approach your time with the Holy Spirit in quietness, which is exactly what **Principle 1** and **Principle 2** will help you attain.

Remember the Holy Spirit is courteous and does not operate effectually in strife. Therefore, when you begin to implement **Principle 1** and **Principle 2**, you will be modeling **Principle 3** before your grieving loved one. As previously discussed, God has not and will not leave nor forsake any of His children, especially during times of despair. The application of **Principle 3** will bring you more confidence and boldness as you intercede. You will become better at noticing and hearing the Holy Spirit, who has all authority through God's infallible Word (John 14:16-17c). The quieter you become, the closer you will be to receiving the best help available for all who believe.

If doubt ever arises, read John 16:13, which states, "Howbeit when he, the Spirit of truth, is come, he will guide you into all truth: for he shall not speak of himself; but whatsoever he shall hear, *that* shall he speak: and he will shew you things to come." This means all information flowing from the Holy Spirit is heard from our omnipotent and omnipresent God. That's deep. Your call to join this journey operates best when under the guidance and watchful care of the Holy Spirit.

Deeper Look at Principle 4: The Journey Belongs to Your Grieving Loved One

Principle 4 is the relationship gatekeeper. **The journey belongs to your grieving loved one**. Although **Principle 4** in theory is easy enough, it is the root cause of most grief-related communication and relationship hurdles. The best course of action is to maintain confidentiality and privacy at all costs. Sometimes, the loss touches in a way that might require you, as with Courtney and I, to share hats. Although times were few, sometimes even Courtney, "my rock," needed me too. During these times, Courtney's crisis took center and my roles had to temporarily switch. This meant Dr. Jacqueline Phelps had to learn, and is still learning, how to master goodly Simon.

As the supporter, it is important to observe with the commitment and confidence to seek God's assistance and trust it above all else. Only deviating if and when led by your wisdom and intimate knowledge of your grieving loved one's current atmosphere, including triggers and milestones.. Please understand, it is never wrong to seek help. Although your commitment and dedication is to walk with the griever spiritually, God provides many resources. The infallible Word provides many examples of God using secular means for the good of His children. Sometimes it might take more—and that is okay. Your assistance cannot comfort, pray away, or adequately manage the signs and symptoms of complicated grief. We do not fear. We remain watchful for the signs and symptoms of complicated grief, which may include, but are not limited to:

- Focus on little else but your loved one's death
- Intense sorrow, pain, and rumination over the loss of your loved one
- Intense and persistent longing or pining for the deceased
- Numbness or detachment
- Problems accepting the death
- Bitterness about your loss
- Feeling life holds no meaning or purpose
- Lack of trust in others
- Inability to enjoy life or think back on positive experiences with your loved one.

Although we understand, there are situations that require temporary prescribed assistance to cope. We still align and then bring all under the authority of God. This book is a gentle assistive tool. All healing and acceptance flow from our shared experiences and wisdom as believers in Christ Jesus. It is only through His blood we have the power and access to call those things that are not into existence. Therefore, the takeaway here is, even if we are prescribed medication or treatment, God's desire is for us to bring everything to Him.

Just as you have come to trust the Holy Spirit is speaking to you through the pages of this book, please trust He desires to lead you, too. If complicated grief does arrive, trust the professionals and continue growing yourself in the Word. As we discussed earlier, some things are simply situational and beyond our physical control. You must not lean to your own understanding, but rather trust what the Father has given us in His infallible Word. You must be committed and ready, which simply means to stay in the Word of God, never ceasing to remember to pray and to acknowledge the Father in all His ways. The implementation of **Principle 4** will help to safeguard your grief supporter relationship just as with Jesus and Simon of Cyrene. Just keep working all four Principles.

Now we have completed our deeper looks, we can begin discussing our selected seven stages or phases of grief: shock, denial, anger, guilt, sorrow and depression, acceptance, and engagement. Each stage or phase will be discussed independently and collectively (transitional blending), starting with Chapter 1: Shock.

CHAPTER 1

Shock

Shock is a built-in protection mechanism. It kicks in to protect someone from the initial feelings of being completely overwhelmed. When circumstances or events are too devastating, shock provides the temporary emotional protection or space needed for the body to adjust. There is no magical formula to move someone on from shock. Shock is normal. The griever may say they're "feeling numb," or you may observe them experiencing "blankness" where they seem to be on autopilot. For me, shock was frightening and numbing because of the nothingness. Some grievers experience an inability to cry. Others may not be able to stop crying. All emotions or lack of emotions are welcomed during these initial moments of realignment and adjustment.

Like all stages of grief, the foggy, numbing realization of shock is the body's protective mechanism. I remember going to sleep the night Michela passed over. It was the best sleep I can ever remember receiving. I remember waking up beside Courtney, both of us astonished that we had been able to fall asleep. We were even more surprised with how rested we both felt. I truly believe this was a direct result of so many saints praying on our behalf. The fervent, heartfelt prayers of our loved ones interceding on our behalf that night truly helped us.

We limit ourselves as believers when we do not utilize all the weapons the Father has provided for His children. I believe that as word spread of Michela's passing over that night, hundreds of friends and family members stayed up and prayed. This allowed Courtney and me to rest as never before. You can trust this truth: "The effectual fervent prayer of a righteous man availeth much" (James 5:16b, KJV). I have come to trust the truth of that tragic night. The fervent prayers of the righteous, those whom God had already made righteous, ushered Courtney and me to a place of peaceful rest. It was a surpassing understanding type of peace, one the situation would have attempted to steal from us that first night. It is this type of power that I'm encouraging you to tap into without ceasing. This journey will require you to immediately begin to implement, sharpen, and continue using the tools of spiritual warfare. As someone who was the recipient of a peaceful rest that still surpasses my understanding (Philippians 4:7), it is my prayerful hope that you will begin and/or continue to never cease from praying for those who are mourning, that they may be comforted. We never cease from praying because the duration and magnitude of grief-based shock is different for everyone.

Sharing the Weight of Grief

Like David and Job, we all question at times. We might ask ourselves, "Where is God? Does He not hear my cries?" No one's heart is exempted. We can take a deeper look into the affairs of the heart through the words of Job to his three friends that we discussed previously, or through the words of David, who cried out to God for the life of his child with Bathsheba. Although David was a man after God's own heart, the heartache associated with the thought of losing his newly born son brought him to his knees. The Bible explains in 2 Samuel 12:15–17 how David fasted and laid on the ground all night. The numbing and paralyzing shock had brought David to a place where even the elders and David's family were concerned for his safety. In Psalm 51, David's anguish over the circumstance he finds in his heart is compelling and offers us a glimpse of his great lamentation. This should provide comfort and encouragement to those of us who believe. It will hopefully inspire those who might be reading this book with a skeptical heart to maybe consider reaching out to God for His help. He is willing and ready to receive all who call on His wonderful name. Just as with David and Job, questions will arise for the person you are blessed to be supporting. It is okay. As the supporter, your assistance does not require you to be God, Jesus, or the Holy Spirit. How could your words ever be more beneficial than those of the Mighty Comforter? How can we answer supernatural questions with finite reasoning? At our best we are only vessels being used by the Father to deliver a message of healing, love, and comfort to a heart that feels like its hope has been deferred (Proverbs 13:12).

One of the most apparent signs of shock is questioning. I truly believe that the Father's perfect design for humanity allows us to have free will, as it is through free will that we have our creative desires. Shock places the brain and the heart out of alignment. Your grieving loved one is heartsick at the same time as the brain is in a state of questioning. Questioning is a permissible temporary need. It allows the brain time to catch up with the heart, or vice versa. The questions might flow from the heart at one moment: "Why does my heart hurt so bad?" or "How could God hurt me so badly?" Then five minutes later, the questions might flow from the head: "How could she be sliding down a waterslide one minute and then gone the next?" It is during these questioning times that you the supporter must trust the truth and the assurances given to us in God's Word as you apply our **Principles.** God has always allowed His children to come to Him with their needs and questions. The Father patiently allowed me to question Him for months before moving me along my journey. All references in my life had been immediately turned upside down. It is my humble opinion that He understood the depth of despair I was experiencing. "And now these three remain: faith, hope, and love. But the greatest of these is love" (1 Corinthians 13:13, NIV). With love being something so great and precious to God, we can expect Him to provide help and understand exactly how we are and what we need during these initial shock-filled moments. He will answer all questions in His perfect timing.

Your only position should be the steadfast and discerning implementation of **Principle 1:** "The work belongs to God," **Principle 2:** "Silence is more than okay, it is vital," and **Principle 3:** "The Holy Spirit is the master teacher." These will pull your shocked loved one closer and closer toward a deeper intimacy with the great Comforter. As well, keep in mind **Principle 4:** "The journey belongs to your grieving loved one." The main goal here is to steadfastly love one another (John 13:34). This can exhibit itself differently in the life of a grieving believer, as we sometimes unintentionally become more and more withdrawn.

Over the years of my grief journey, I have come to witness many spirit-filled believers who are over-concerned with how a breakdown or outburst might be viewed by others. Of course, I believe that everyone gets to determine their own healthy path to travel. But for my part, I let my grief come as it will, whenever and wherever it falls: at church, in the grocery store, or while in the middle of a conversation. If the Spirit calls, I answer, and most of the time my witness is public. How else would I have been able to answer the Father's call to write this book? I believe that this was and is my best course of action, and it has served me well. Nevertheless, as a supporter, it is important for you to understand: just because your grieving loved one teaches Sunday school or is a minister, this does not exempt them from experiencing all the stages and phases of grief. Their initial road is just as shocking, numbing, or despairing as anyone else's. As Job requested of his three friends, we must allow those in mourning the space to hear God. The voice of the Holy Spirit will never lead us wrong. We should never mistakenly assume that too many or not enough tears equates toward any level of faith. As the supporter, your goal is to surrender all work to God and to remember His strength is made perfect in your weakness (2 Corinthians 12:9, KJV).

Be ready to quietly usher in peace during times of outward grief expression. Statements such as "everything will be okay" might only elicit more of the same. Instead, try using words such as "it's okay, let it out." These words, although almost the same, are completely different in the heart and mind of a griever. The statement "everything will be okay" may only bring up more questions within the griever's overworked mind. The words "it's okay, let it out" provide room and welcome surrenderance. Be poised and ready to provide gentle, accepting statements each time you are blessed to witness an outburst of emotional tears from your griever. These are wonderful opportunities to gently model your **Principles** and trust without preaching or providing your own thoughts and ways. Your griever will eventually begin to listen more closely to the soft, gentle voice of the Holy Spirit. The takeaway for this section is that shock is normal and healthy in the mind, heart, and soul of a griever. The duration or magnitude is determined by the griever. Your loving responses to the griever during these times will usher them toward the only true answer during our times of suffering: Jesus Christ. He and only He can deliver the desired soundness of mind and garments of praise that are available to all who come to Him for comfort.

TRANSITORY BLENDING PHASE

For the purpose of cohesion and clarity, I utilized the most typical signs and symptoms associated with known characteristics of grief. I also provide conversation in terms of stages and phases. Nevertheless, it is important to always remember that a grieving heart does not operate in neat, compartmentalized phases. Therefore, after each stage, we will discuss transitory moments, days, or even years. These transitory periods are experienced by all mourners as potential growth, growth that moves us to and through our journey with grief. Although personal and fluid, absolutely no one is exempt from the shock, denial, anger, guilt, and sorrow which accompany loss. I can remember in the past watching other grievers and proclaiming, "I would never say or do certain things." Now, eighteen years later, I *have* done and said it all. I think it was just impossible for me to understand something or define something that I had absolutely no point of reference for. And then, once I did have that point of reference, it was almost like the affliction was so great, I needed time before I could see the answers I so desperately yearned to receive.

Times of blending are truly times of great confusion in the heart and mind of your grieving loved one. The Word teaches that "many are the afflictions of the righteous: but the Lord delivereth him out of them all" (Psalm 34:19, KJV). You can look at your grieving loved one's heart as a treasure that is currently consumed in overwhelming pain—a pain which might hinder its ability to recognize God's deliverance. You, the supporter, the observer, the eyes and ears of God, will be better equipped to diligently seek God's guidance to comfort ye one to another. You have been selected by the Father to be seated exactly where prayer will be needed in every stage. Please be extremely careful here, mindful that Father's desired journey for His children has both afflictions and blessings. Remember, like with Courtney, that this truth might be too much for your grieving loved one at this stage. Through the guidance of the Holy Spirit, you will learn when to speak. You will learn when to be silent. If you patiently wait on God, He will give you the words to say at every hour they are needed.

You will become a master concerning your loved one's unique grief phases and stages. In due time, you will speak and your grieving loved one's heart will begin to soften. As His children, we appreciate and accept the Father's truths regardless of the phase or stage. He has given us the ability to overcome them all. It is during these transitory blending phases when your grieving loved one might exhibit even more signs and symptoms, signs such as not eating or sleeping, or symptoms such as loss or gain of weight. Transitions are perfectly okay. You will see them often over the course of this journey. Trust the truth and apply your **Principles.** The appearance of signs and symptoms is an indicator that God is doing the work. Breathe and continue to apply the **Principles.**

I believe that denial, the next stage, was easier to write about than shock, maybe because reliving the shock of those immediate moments, hours, days, and years takes me immediately back to my initial pains. I somehow became accustomed to holding my breath or waiting for the next shoe to fall. Maybe, even through the preparation of writing this book, I am still uncovering uncharted waters on this journey. Perhaps this is why, even after so much time has passed, I can be brought right back to the day Michela passed over. Remembering will sometimes escort your griever toward the uneasiness of attempting to understand through questioning. It is during these times when they might share feelings of being overwhelmed, or feeling stuck in mud or foggy, which will usher them into dealing with the present. But life will undoubtedly cause them to have to deal with normalcies such as having to take a shower, brushing their teeth, remembering trash day is Wednesday, or returning to work.

Life will continue. Your grieving loved one will be gently and sometimes violently brought face to face with God's truth: all seasons pass, and time stops for no one. During this time as the supporter, your fervent prayers should be mainly focused on calling forth fruits of the Spirit, saying things such as "we bless You, Father, as we surrender to Your will," "thank you, Father, for your peace," or "bless Your Holy Name; we accept Your rest." These types of short prayers will make it easy to never cease from praying.

I can remember not being able to pray during the initial stages of grief. The words just would not formulate. Other days, the pain would be so intense, I could only say His name, "Jesus." As you support your loved one, trust in the truth, the living Word of God, the finished work of Jesus' blood on the cross, and the spoken promises of the Holy Spirit. As you come to trust these truths, the power of intercession will have its perfect way. During this time, your grieving loved one's mind will be overstimulated and fatigued. They will be operating on autopilot, making phone calls to family and friends, preparing eulogies, selecting burial clothing, and buying plots. This is why shock or feelings of numbness are temporarily beneficial. Many grievers describe it as a supernatural empowerment to complete tasks which seem impossible, tasks like going to view the body. It has to be done. I had to go. And trust me, I was on autopilot. These events have a way of escorting a grieving heart violently into the present. It is during this time that many people will be around. It is okay to temporarily fade into the background. The Holy Spirit will give you the perfect timing to come along beside your grieving loved one. When the crowds lessen, when the dirt has been laid, and when people have returned to their own daily concerns, the Holy Spirit will guide you back to service. Until then, position yourself in steadfast and discerning prayer and follow the **Principles**. During this brief absence, rest as you allow **Principle 4** to take full root, taking comfort in the progressive facts. Life will gently remind your grieving loved one when it is time to move just a little forward.

The shock of Michela being gone, and gone forever, did subside. But it delivered me unknowingly (at the time) toward even more questions and unrest. It is during this time in my grief that I accepted denial as my comforter.

CHAPTER 2
Denial

Denial offers temporary relief and comfort. In this stage, some people deny their loved one has actually passed away. Others deny how deeply affected they are by the loss, saying things like "God has a plan" and "all things happen for the good," when in actuality they are still devastated. As an observant supporter, during these initial assessments, your grieving loved one's responses are less of an indicator of how they are doing and more of an opportunity for you to observe their nonverbal body communications and behaviors.

By this point, the shock of the news or set of events has lessened. There is now space to question. These questions bring the pain front and center, especially once the funeral has been concluded and the flowers have started slowly fading and turning brown. The initial support "peripherals" are less and less available. For the purpose of this book, we will term as *peripherals* those who are available during the first few weeks, but are soon pulled away due to their lives. They may be pulled away by very legitimate reasons, such as physical or emotional limitations (our brothers were hurting too much to help us), geographical restraints (our parents lived in another state), or work and school schedules (everyone's schedules were just as busy as mine). The pressures of their own schedules make it difficult for even the most dedicated of peripherals to support the griever. But despite the fact that these are all valid reasons, it can still feel to the griever like they're being left behind. The real truth is that even ministers find it difficult to manage the affairs of the bereaved, and every grieving heart must come to grips with the fact that time stops for no one.

When Michela passed over, I was in my first year at UT Southwestern Medical in Dallas Texas. As a wife, a mother of two, an employee at American Airlines, and a full-time physical therapy student, my plate was full to the brim. But this was my normal. It was what all the "wonder women" were doing, working that thing. Nevertheless, as I soon came to learn, time does not stop for anyone, and it would not be stopping for me. Although inside I was screaming "stop," "slow down," and "can we take one moment," I came to learn that no matter how traumatically devastating the circumstances, you either keep up or get left behind.

The university's allied health program allowed medical students seven bereavement days. On the seventh day you had to have your butt in class or take a leave of absence. But "leave of absence" meant "quit"—or at least that's how I received it. Quit? Absolutely not. I had already lost so much. The least God could do was give me this. So, the Monday after the funeral, I was back in classes. This was my reality during the initial weeks and months after Michela's home-going celebration. Therefore, my approach to her passing was mixed with secular head sense. My mind had been so engulfed in secular science—studying how the body works and dissecting cadavers—that it would not allow my heart to receive Michela's corpse, or even stand to look at it. It was not her, just a void of life shell. I would say things like, "I'm okay. What would it change if I wasn't?" Just as your grieving loved one might, I would say in my head, "I have no choice; I have to be okay." But I had no earthly clue what *okay* meant anymore. I would also over-spiritualize my hurt, saying things like "Absent from the body is present with the Lord" so I could move through my day. But I was still spiritually stuck. It was a kind of emotional paralysis. While everyone else seemed to be dealing with time, time was not my friend. It terrified me. Would I forget her voice? Would her smell slowly fade away from all of those sealed ziplock bags I had saved of her clothing? Would everyone else forget Michela's breathtaking smile?

As unique individuals, everyone has different approaches to dealing with these types of questions. This is perfectly okay. There are no wrongs or rights here! We are all finding our way, pressing through the journey which will one day give rise to truths we can trust. Now, blessed with hindsight and a fuller revelation of God's living Word over my journey, I can truly attest that during the first five years of Michela's passing over, there were many seasons of moving out of shock (numbness) to denial (unbelief), only to find myself subtly or violently thrust right back there again and again. I felt like the main character in a *Groundhog Day* horror movie. During these seasons, it felt like I was stuck in mud. I could see the mud. I could feel the mud overtaking me. But each day's routine would start and end the exact same way: me up to my neck in muddy overwhelming pain and anguish.

Today, thank you, Jesus, I can see more clearly. Just as your grieving loved one will one day proclaim, I have made it to the unknown finish line. The seemingly never-ending treadmill race has concluded. But for now, you must trust the Father and my testimony. You must stand, interceding, at the finish line. Please understand, your grieving loved one may feel as if they're on a treadmill stuck on rewind, feeling like their arms and legs aren't moving. Through the lens of your grieving loved one, everyone else, the peripherals, seem to be moving purposefully and with ease on their treadmills. Their limbs are all intact. Their treadmill dashboards are fully operational. Your grieving loved will begin to say or exhibit signs of being forgotten or left behind. They would love to move faster, or even simply get off of this horrible ride. But their limbs are not working and their treadmill dashboard is broken. When they try to run, their legs do not move.

Sharing the Weight of Grief

When they try to pull the emergency stop switch on their treadmill, it speeds up. It is during these times when you must trust God's understanding and abilities to do above what you can think or ask. Trust God's power to control the mud and the treadmill of our journeys. You don't have doubt or walk in uncertainty. When you feel compelled by the Spirit, move quickly. You are ready. Remember the **Principles** and move into prayerful obedience.

Before beginning my grief journey, I never really gave much notice to the stages of grief. I learned them in college and even referenced them during conversations with my clients and patients. But I never incorporated myself into the conversation because I was not a pitiful victim. This is the type of resistance you might encounter when you first try to help. Just breathe. Each time you will become more and more equipped through the leading of the Holy Spirit.

For a long time, I resisted anything resembling acceptance in my own life. But when it came to Erica . . . well. Maybe. Perhaps? I would give it a try. Soon after Michela's funeral, we were referred to the WARM Place, a grief support center for families of grieving children. Although I loved it for Courtney and Erica, I absolutely hated grouping with the "always tearing" women's group. They seemed to be such pitiful looking and sounding people. Nope, absolutely not. I could stomach taking Erica to her group, for children whose siblings have passed over. But, I thought, why do the parents have to meet? I didn't need to wear a "Look at Me, My Child Died" badge or sign. Most of all, I didn't need anything pressing or pulling me away from my alone time with Michela's memories.

If interviewed during those very uncertain times, I would have insisted I was the only grief expert in the room. I have come to understand, I was in complete denial. The glorifying truth that can be trusted is Father and His angels were encompassing me. They fed and watered me. They kept me safe by blocking some of my pains until I could start to face them. It is during this season in which the Father began to supernaturally quench my thirst of unanswerable questioning. Like a skillful surgeon, He began to carve away all of the dead, decaying tissue. The Holy Spirit will lead you at the exact time if, like Simon, you have your eyes and ears attuned to His timing and are willing.

Your grieving loved one may experience additional traumas from other interactions on their journey of grief.

One such example for me was the young ER doctor's callous statement "she expired." I remember not being able to understand what *expired* meant. It seemed like hours passed from the time the words escaped his lips to the moment his raw and very insensitive analysis landed in my heart. I can remember sitting in Arlington Memorial Hospital ER's private waiting room beside Courtney, trying to focus, while at the same time denying the reality which sat before me. Only God can help heal these types of trauma. The apparent pains caused by the death and the collateral pains caused by everything else.

Imagine the denial that your grieving loved one experiences the first time they see the lifeless body lying before them. It is an image I will never forget. Michela's lifeless body, lying there. Void of life. Violently snatched from me. Remember how we previously discussed how life would escort your grieving loved one, sometimes violently, into the present? This was one of those moments. I could not deny that Michela as I had come to love her would be no more. In the same way, if you are quiet and patiently wait on the Lord, reality will eventually pull and press your grieving loved one forward. The fast forward of my next morning was totally different. This is yet another fact concerning grieving: the stages and phases are fleeting at times. As they rush in like waves, subtly disappearing and reappearing. Because I would wake up and be so overwhelmed with grief, I decided it would be more beneficial to just think differently. I secretly decided to pretend that Michela was just at asthma camp. It was denial on steroids. I can't remember exactly when I started resting in this lie, but according to my journal, it was after the funeral (the peripherals had all returned to their normal lives) and before school had restarted (mid-August). The timeframe was already around the time that Michela went to Cook Children's Asthma Camp every year. All the key components were in place. So let the real denial begin . . .

It began innocently enough; whenever the enemy or my emotions would tell me "she's gone," I would immediately tell myself, "No, she's at camp." And I would immediately be okay. This temporarily permissible state of denial gave my body and mind longer moments of rest. Not peace, just rest. Michela loved camp. So, thoughts concerning camp temporarily loosened the grip of grief. Although it is not beneficial to take up roots in this type of denial, looking back, I would have to consider this stage my most welcoming to enter—which is also why it was my most stifling to give up and pass on from.

It is important to remember your grieving loved one may or may not have exactly the same experiences. They could visit denial briefly during the initial moments or not at all. Instead of focusing too heavily on identifying the stage of grief (i.e. whether it's shock and/or denial), open your heart and ears so you can carefully listen to and observe your grieving loved one's patterns. Patterns which seem off balance must be addressed if they place anyone in harm's way. However, if there is no harm, your position must be to intercede, not to intervene.

For me, during this part of my journey I was very comfortable with denial. It reached the point where I would rather spend time with the dead in Christ Jesus, with memories of Michela's life, than with the living: my daughter Erica, who was only five at the time. I would get upset if anyone made me feel uneasy or distracted me from my sole purpose: daily honoring the memory of Michela.

Sharing the Weight of Grief

I denied or refused to go to, deal with, or engage in anything daring to come against my chosen truth at that time. Grief-based denial affects all parts of your grieving loved one's life. At the time Michela passed over, if asked at what level I would consider my faith, I would have foolishly given a quantitative answer equating to "great," "strong," or "healthy." After over eighteen years on this journey, I have realized that faith is best measured after it has been tried and tested. This testing is meant not to harm us, but to move us toward God's expected end. Unfortunately, oftentimes, at least for the believer, this means afflictions, afflictions which lead us kicking and screaming toward unpaved journeys with no guide. Peripherals who had not lost a child could not be trusted and were quickly and silently shut down in my head. What did they know? Peripherals who had the unfortunate luck to be ahead of me on their grief journeys would have their words dissected quietly. I would unravel their words in my head. Even if they had buried a child, like me, their pain could not be as overwhelming or as painful as my life was without my beloved Michela.

Denial comes easy after the passing of a child; after all, who wants to think about or wear those shoes? That was where Courtney, Erica, and I found ourselves—broken, no longer four, now a forced three. It was simply easier on everyone to just believe that Michela was at a sleepover or over at my brother's house. By envisioning that Michela was just not home and would soon be returning, my overstimulated brain and unruly emotions could temporarily find space to complete my daily tasks. It was during those first few months that denial temporarily allowed me to get up out of the bed, brush my teeth, and tend to my family. Denial became my friend, because it would gently say, "it's okay. She's at camp, just like every summer," or "it's okay, she's at church," or "at AWANAs."

Denial gave me temporary sanctuary from my pain. God only knows how He pulled me through. I can remember talking to Michela in the house, speaking to her as though she was present. I can remember, on the first day of school, neatly setting her clothes out. You know how mothers and daughters match up the latest fads? I was matching her bow with her socks, just as we had done together so many times before. All of this was done in secret, including buying the brand-new backpack hidden in the hatchback of my car. When Erica asked, "Mommy, who's that for?" I told her I would be blessing someone who needed it and could not afford one. The reality was, I was nowhere near reality. Denial was my dearest and most intimate friend. And the backpack was absolutely for Michela.

What made denial so comforting for me? It never passed judgment or pressed back. Denial is the friend who never disagrees with you, no matter what the situation. Denial assured me Michela would love the backpack, and, magically, the conversation would stop there. Denial assured me it was okay to choose to stay in the past with Michela versus life with Erica. Spending time with denial meant Michela was alive and well. Denial allowed me to eat, sleep, comb Erica's hair, and, yes, go school shopping. As silly as it may sound, it comforted me. The only truth I allowed myself at that time was denial. It temporarily eased my pain. Denial gave me the strength to go places that reminded me of my loss, such as church, youth choir practice, and communion. Denial told me everything was okay. Denial gave my mind and heart time to almost catch up to one another. So, yes, your grieving loved one might seem to be in deep denial. As the supporter, this is a time to silently observe and pray. No one would have been able to take Michela's backpack out of my hands. No one would have been able to make me realize just how much in denial I truly was. I had come to trust and agree with denial.

Living in denial or taking up permanent residence in denial is not beneficial and should be referred to a grief professional. The healthy kind of denial, the type I am referring to, is not chronic. It is survival. Your grieving loved one might not be able to come face to face with every truth at once, especially during the early stages of their grief journey, like when I was shopping for school supplies in early August. Therefore, as you assess your grieving loved one's state of denial, prayerfully remember that during the first few months, denial can provide a temporary space to rest. Denial stopped the overwhelming voices of impossibilities, allowing me to stay in Walmart with all the back-to-school sounds, smells, and memories. It allowed me to buy school supplies for Erica.

I can remember not being able to face the truth because the truth took my breath away. I can remember choosing denial, because my trust in God was being challenged, just as Job's was. During those early moments and days, I went to work, church, the store, school, and everywhere else life forced me to attend while secretly being comforted by temporarily needed denial. While living in denial, I would begin almost every day the same way. I would open my eyes and immediately hear, "it's true; she's gone." This would usually cause me to run out the door and down the street, with or without shoes. I would run until I tired myself out. The flight would eventually give way to exhaustion. Courtney would follow me in the car, pick me up, and then escort me safely home. Once home, Courtney would leave for work and I would begin my day of denial.

You might ask, how or when did I ever move from such a close relationship with denial? At first, I truly believed that the infallible Word of God came and snatched me out, but after researching through my old journals for this book, I now understand it was the Holy Spirit. He convinced me of the possibility of a better way. He began by just softly suggesting that a day with less pain and anguish was possible. This continued for months, according to my journal. God used butterflies, sermons, patients at a senior living facility, and even my dreams to confirm that He was able and willing to help me. Over a series of events and time, I began to lean more toward a defiant, almost cocky attitude of, "Okay. Maybe, on Your Word, I might give it a try!" I unknowingly stopped standing in agreement with denial and began standing on the possibilities of the Father. Hallelujah to the Lamb. I truly believe this is when the Father sent in His special forces unit: Pastor Joyce Myers.

THE JOYCE MYERS STORY

Michela passed over in the summer of 2003, only a few weeks after her sixth-grade graduation. My close relationship with denial was at full force at the beginning of the 2003–04 school year. Erica was entering first grade at Mount Olive Baptist Charter School, the same school Michela had attended since kindergarten, which also happened to be connected to our home church. The first few months of the school year, I would drop Erica off at school, pretending all was well with my soul, then return home every single day and go back to bed.

One morning, I returned home, hopped in bed, and accidentally hit the remote. Up on the television popped the most peculiar-sounding woman. I remember saying, "A woman in the pulpit! What would Reverend say?" At the time of Michela's passing over, we were blessed to be members of Mount Olive Baptist Church under the beloved late Pastor N. L. Robinson. Pastor Myers's voice snatched my attention because Southern Baptists did not ordain women and I was not accustomed to women preachers. Therefore, Pastor, Minister, and Evangelist

Joyce Myers immediately stirred my interest. But while this brief initial encounter mostly sparked curiosity and disbelief, it was enough to allow some truth to seep down into my soul from God. It was as if, without my permission, the Holy Spirit and Joyce Myers came into agreement on my situation. I can remember Pastor Myers saying, "It is a choice. God is not going to get tired or change His mind. Even if you lay in that bed until you stink to high heaven." My journal provides a clear record of the defiant nature of my back talk. I would come home, get back in the bed, pull the covers over my head, and willingly choose to reject God. I would write in my journal, "Then fine! I choose to lay in my bed and stink!"

My journal entries go cold and then pick back up approximately three weeks after Pastor Myers's introduction into my situation. I continued to come home, get back in the bed, pull the covers over my head, and mourn. Then, one day, it just did not feel good anymore. I thought, "Okay, this is not working." I began to watch Joyce instead of just lying in the bed. Could God really use this middle-aged female pastor to minister to me? Pastor Myers was in direct conflict with what I believed and had been taught. I can remember thinking, "If I was wrong about this, what else have I been wrong about?" It was like her presence challenged my soul to fight. I began to believe that maybe there could be the slight possibility of moments without discomfort. I started to wonder, was denial, or my love affair with denial, hindering me from even imagining peace again?

No one knew I was denying Michela had passed over. I said the right things at the right time. Tears, check! Anger, check! Doubt, check! It was like everything I knew had been turned inside out in one day. Nothing looked the same and nothing felt the same. So it became really easy to just "choose," as Joyce had so crudely put it. For several months, I continued to watch Pastor Myers, mocking her and God. He so graciously allowed me to question Him in shock and refuse His version of the truth in denial. Denial was loving and comforting. It did not come up against my pain. I would feel pain, and denial would gently say, "Oh, she's at a friend's house," and the pain would temporarily lessen. But there was something in Pastor Myers's message that provoked my soul. I would hear Joyce's strong, authoritative voice say, "It's a choice. You get to choose." One day her words became silly. I was listening to one of her sermons and realized I was being ministered to by a full-fledged woman pastor. I started to think, "If God can use a woman to speak into my soul, then maybe, just maybe . . . I can be healed." From that day forward, God continued to reveal his love, protection, and desire for me to trust Him instead of my denial.

This is why it is so important as the supporter for you to have a rich life of prayer and supplication as you intercede on behalf of your grieving loved one. As you intercede on their behalf, trust God's words in Romans

8:27, that He who searches our hearts knows better than you. This will help you to yield up your ways, thoughts, anxieties, and cares to Him. Who would have known that the Father would use my spirit of religiosity and belief in complementarianism to bring me to Pastor Myers? He placed me exactly where He wanted me first. I say *first* because this is where we miss the mark. Let's take me, for instance: if you had been my supporter and found out I had been pretending Michela was at camp, as well as purchasing a backpack and every supply on the seventh grade supply list; if you knew I came home every day after dropping Erica off at school and returned to bed until it was time to pick her up; if you knew some days I would sit and smell Michela's dirty clothes for hours—if you knew all of this, would you have been able to quietly allow me to continue? Or would you have suggested that I be committed for psychoanalysis, or at the very least, suggested a loving intervention with Courtney to ensure my sanity? But God instead challenged me from my bed. He met me right in my stink-filled bed, saying, "Will you trust Me even when what I am asking you to do seems impossible and comes from the mouth of a woman pastor?" When He used Pastor Myers, whose authoritative posture managed to capture me right there, lying in the bed with denial, I didn't have to go anywhere. I didn't have to change my stance, or even believe. God did it all! He decided on the message and the messenger. He knew I would immediately question her right to even suggest she understood my pain. After all, she was not even supposed to be delivering messages. I would lie in bed and cynically analyze her sermons. Gotcha! God was not only strategic, but also full of wisdom, as He knew exactly how to challenge my disbelieving brokenness. Like a master of my broken heart, God touched my unbelief at just the right moment, using the most unlikely source. He inserted possibility.

It is important for you to surrender your natural need to remove your grieving loved one from the process. You will have to lean deep into the infallible Word, press even harder in prayer, and flower yourself around those whom the Father has placed around you. These types of relationships—family, friends, congregation, accountability partners, or even a support group—are very beneficial. Use healthy, confidential, fully matured conversation when sharing. As the overseer and the one who is able to see more clearly at this season in the journey, it is important that you trust the truth and hold onto the promises of God. You must know, without a doubt, that the same power that raised Jesus from the dead is available here. You must be willing to fight this battle with all the spiritual warfare tools the Father teaches us to use. You must be willing to lean not to your own understanding, or grief perception of your grieving loved one. You can and must trust the truth. God has not been taken by surprise by our temporary situation. Just the opposite; He has been continuing and will continue His good work until the day of Jesus (Philippians 1:6).

I do not know the strategy the Father will use to bring your loved one to the fullness of Who He Is, but He promises us in His Word to never leave us nor forsake us (Deuteronomy 31:6). The Father knows the agonizing pain of watching His only beloved Son pass over. He has already accomplished what you are committing to embark upon. It is now your faith and the faith of your grieving loved one which He is cultivating in the image of His only begotten Son. You can be sure, just as with me, that the Master Creator knows exactly who to send on His behalf, and when and where that should be. Just as my television just happened to be on Joyce Myers the very day she delivered the perfect message "It's a Choice," a.k.a., why are you still lying in bed stinking to high heaven sermon? He will strategically bring your grieving loved one comfort during this time. He will use the most unique and peculiar resources to turn His children toward His face.

I will forever be grateful for Pastor Joyce Myers and her saving message to me. I am thankful God refused to share my heart with denial. Every believer, including your grieving loved one, will have to look into the infallible Word of God and choose whom they will serve. I am a living testimony: the Father is a good parent, the kind who does not allow any of His children to deny Him as Lord. He will bring down every imagination and stronghold that dares to separate Him from one of His children. Just as with me, God will use any person, place, or thing to show Himself strong in our lives. Just as I did, your grieving loved one might develop a temporary permissible relationship with denial. Trust me, God will bring down every imagination which attempts to exalt itself as Lord, including denial. Just as he used by boastful prideful attitude to draw me into relationship with Pastor Myers. He will restore, bring, or create all your grieving loved one's needs to choose whom and what they will believe. These are the beginning stages of possibilities, when a hope-deferred broken heart starts to consider or reconsider that perhaps there's a slim chance there might be a less painful way. Your grieving loved one might not visit denial in front of you, or at all. Being observant and ready to pray is the best position when interceding for this type of hurt and pain. I am here today because of prayer and supplication. It is through prayer and supplication Jesus made it through His journey. If we, therefore, have the same power as Jesus, we must believe the Word of God can stand tall against any levels of denial. You can trust the truth that our Father will complete what He has begun until the day of Jesus Christ. No matter how temporarily permissible denial might be for a weary and overworked mind. No matter how much of an immediate shield it gives from piercing anguish. We must hold to the truth, God will bring everything captive that dares to stand against His Word and will for the lives of His children (2 Corinthians 10:5). Let me just stop to once again acknowledge God, my Father, for breaking my relationship with denial.

As we move into or out of any phase or stage, we must remember to refrain from seeking our own desires and ways. For example, let us assume your grieving loved one has a grief anniversary fast approaching. (This is a date you *will* need to take care to remember.) You think it would be a good idea to plan some type of event or celebration in remembrance or memorialization. Research on grief best practices suggests being proactive reduces the stress on or around dates of significance, like birth and death dates. Most facilitators would encourage being proactive with intentional planning. While at the same time being comfortable with the fact your grieving loved one might not be on board, change their mind at the last moment, or flat out refuse to participate. The slippery slopes of denial can open up personal conversations of doubt for the best of supporters. Questions like "what if I push too hard and my grieving loved one shuts down?" On the other hand, "what if I'm not pushing hard enough and my grieving loved one is home lonely needing a friend?" Both questions are rooted in doubt and control. Which means neither is true. When doubt arises, we acknowledge its presence as we quickly take those thoughts captive, placing them under the Infallible Word of God.

My closest supporters would call me an over-the-top controller, with my favorite statements usually being "I'm okay" or "I've got it." Therefore, planning something to assist me in dealing with a fast-approaching date was difficult at best. To make matters even worse, I'm a bona fide homebody. When things get out of control, I naturally dig in. This is why neither of the above statements were true. If you push too hard, forgive yourself quickly and trust God. If you don't push hard enough, forgive yourself quickly and trust God. Absolutely no one could have convinced me of anything until it was time. Through prayer and observation, the Holy Spirit will provide you with all the tools you need. As long as there is no immediate threat of harm, we should allow the grieving heart its perfect placement on the journey. As you may recall, I was lying in a bed stinking to high heaven when God used Pastor Myers to challenge me. Whether moving from shock, aftershock, or denial, continually revisit **Principle 1** and **Principle 2**. Encourage yourself in how well you have been growing. Don't allow momentary objects of transition to block your view. You are doing one of the most important tasks the Father places before all of those who are called in the preparation of the gospel. This is exactly why relying on **Principle 1** and **Principle 2** is so important. As you continue, please remember no phase or blending of phases can be defined as good or bad, wrong or right, unless the griever is being a threat to themselves or others. As the supporter, posture yourself toward surrendering and allowing your grieving loved one the freedom to move from one emotion to another as you trust the watchful care of the Holy Spirit. This will be extremely important for you to master as we begin to experience even more stages and phases of grief.

Transitory Blending Phase

Emotions will come and go like waves that flood the griever's soul, from denial to anger, or to revisiting shock. As your grieving loved one moves from denial and begins to accept the truth, it can be a very difficult time for their heart. It was like my eyes and ears would be playing tricks on me. Sometimes I could hear Michela and smell her presence about the house. Sometimes I would just forget she had passed over and call to her. Sometimes I would intentionally lead my own broken heart into a place of less painfulness. Other times I would turn on soulful music so I could just sit and cry all day. Regardless of the reasons, the underlying result was a false sense of my current situation. Although some believers will testify to never denying God's truth, I can say, without a doubt, I did.

Denial gave me rest. God allowed me to have this temporary fix until a time He would use pastor Joyce Myers to call me out. It became uncomfortable, turning to yesterday, when day after day nothing changed. Just as Pastor Myers had said, God had refused to change His mind. Michela was not coming back. She was not at a sleepover. She was not at asthma camp. God was gently forcing me to choose whom I would believe.

As your grieving loved one transitions from phase to phase, stage to stage, or question to question, those unstable, permissible denials will have to come face to face with the infallible Word of God. Scriptures they once cherished and trusted to give them guidance are now causing them to spin their wheels. Their imaginations are running wild. This is why only the Holy Spirit can adequately and fully attend to the affairs of man's heart. Remember, He has been strategically positioned right in the middle of their pains and doubts. During seasons of transition, questions resurface. Sometimes these are already-addressed shock questions: How could this happen? Where did I go wrong? Does God not care for me? Or they might be denial questions: How can this be true? Is this a dream? Why do I feel numb? This is why we apply our **Principles** as we patiently await the Father's perfect will for those who mourn. God is requiring your grieving loved one's hope-deferred, broken heart to come, seek, and then receive His will. God knows exactly what lies ahead, whether that be more denial, another day of aftershock, or a blend of both. He intimately knows each of His children, just as He knows every emotion of those who mourn. Trust in the Father's perfected plan. It was designed before your grieving loved one was formed in their mother's womb.

CHAPTER 3

Anger

Anger is a natural, God-given or God-allowed feeling that arises when things within our lives do not go according to our plans. The Word of God teaches us to be slow to anger, because it does not produce the righteousness of God. Well, I was so *angry*. And most of the time, I could not even tell you what I was angry about. This is why, just as with shock and denial, we hold to the promises of the Father that He knows the hearts of His people. Truth is not predicated on our emotional state of being, even if those negative emotions are foolishly being directed toward God. His desire is not to harm us but to give us an "expected end." The exact scripture is, "For I know the thoughts that I think toward you, saith the Lord, thoughts of peace, and not of evil, to give you an expected end" (Jeremiah 29:11, KJV). This is one of my most favorite scriptures. Its relevance is apparent as we go deeper into signs, symptoms, and characteristics commonly associated with grief-related anger.

I love to diligently study Father's Word. Because I'm a seeker, "probing" just comes naturally. When things aren't making sense, my first response is to question. Therefore, when the denial lessened, allowing me to hear Pastor Myers, those innate, natural characteristics started drawing me away from the subtle lure of denial. My heart began to question if scripture really applied to me or my current situation. I questioned if Jeremiah 29:11 really applied to me. Because if I knew nothing else, I absolutely knew living a life without Michela was definitely harmful. Therefore, this meant my favorite scripture in God's Word was not universally applicable. If scripture was not applicable to everyone, then how could it be truth we can trust? These are the kinds of questions your grieving loved one might begin to wrestle with, openly or quietly. I would read scriptures like Psalm 37:4 (KJV), "Delight thyself also in the Lord; and he shall give thee the desires of thine heart," and wonder, was this yet another truth not applicable to me? If I knew anything, it was that this was definitely *not* my desire. I would go even further during my angry temper tantrums. I would violently scream until exhausted because my present and only accepted truth was that God was ignoring me. I was angry at Him that, after my faithful service of bringing Michela to Him, going to Sunday school, and teaching her His thoughts and ways, He would, like one of my enemies, turn His face from me in my time of need. I would demand of God, how could You say that even if I made my bed in hell, You would search me out and find me? Well, here I am, calling out to You with no results after having my heart ripped out of my chest with an old, rusty, jagged blade.

There I stood, grieving over something my Father, the Creator of heaven and earth, had allowed. Mr. "Not the respecter of a person" seemed to be singling me and my family out. Why my daughter? Why me? During my journey with anger, God's thoughts and ways seemed a lot like the opposite of favoritism to me. I could think of a lot more deserving evildoers, all of them more guilty than an eleven-year-old member of His own body of believers. I decided that if He didn't care about me, then I absolutely did not care about Him.

I had just enough Word in me to make myself real, real angry. Angry that God chose me to walk this journey. Angry that other families and their children were safe. Angry because I had to learn how to live my life without Michela, or, at least, so I thought at the time. Angry that God told me "no." Angry at Michela for not telling me how sick she was. Angry at God because Courtney was there when Michela passed over, and I was not. Angry because Erica would not have a sister and would be an only child. Angry because evildoers were allowed to wake up, hurt, and kill, while He was allowing me to be consumed.

My initial reflection before beginning to write this section was, "I believe anger came the most naturally to me." This is because denial gave me permission to do and believe nothing, but anger gave me a job. Being mad and hurt takes a lot of energy. Some grievers might even seem better as they emerge from their beds of self-pity and denial. How could they have known that I was silently boiling over inside? My alone time was no longer spent in bed stinking to high heaven. Now, I would get mad and scream until exhaustion, or drive to the grave site, just to walk the grassy paths at Moore's Funeral Home and declare that God was not hearing me. Most of my anger was directed inwardly toward God and myself. It just seemed so unfair. Michela was my daughter, and I was her mother. How could I not be there? Absolutely *nothing* ever got to my girls without first coming through me. I would ask God, "Why would You disallow me from being there to comfort my child in her time of need?" God, in His wisdom and compassion, granted this privilege to Courtney and to Michela's two oldest uncles instead. I would continue, "Really, the least You could have done was to wait on me." My anger was silently over the top. My accepted truth at that time hinged on my anger. In my heart, I would proclaim, "What a cruel and favoring God we serve!" I know these words are difficult for any believer to hear concerning a God as mighty and powerful as Jehovah. And trust me, they are even difficult to repeat aloud here too. I'm revealing these things to you because you may hear such things pouring from your grieving loved one's hope-deferred heart. You must continue to implement your principles: **Principle 1**: "The work belongs to God;" **Principle 2**: "Silence is more than okay, it is vital;" and **Principle 3**:

"The Holy Spirit is the master teacher." These principles are pulling or pressing us more and more toward our ultimate goal of **Principle 4**: "The journey belongs to your grieving loved one." Knowing God's expected plan, "that all things work together for good to them that love God, to them who are the called according to His purpose" (Romans 8:28, KJV), will melt away all anger in due time.

I silently carried around so much anger, initially at God. I could not understand how He could take Michela when there were so many evil people in this world. How could He take my eleven-year-old daughter? I had diligently followed His child-rearing instructions, taking her to Sunday school, AWANAs, and Vacation Bible School. She loved to be in the house of the Lord. She was kind and compassionate, unlike some of those other kids. Really, I said such awful things. What was it all for? I taught her to respect her elders and to take God's Word to memory. She was supposed to be here with her family. And I had just enough of the Word to know that God chose not to intervene on my behalf. I remember being at Arlington Memorial Hospital, sitting in the ER, holding my Bible. I was so certain that God would give me the desires of my heart. Right? Was He a crazy God? There is no way anyone could get this wrong. My daughter will not die! She will live! I held to that even when they took me to her body, and even on the drive home after the ER doctor coldly informed us that our lovely Michela Brittany had expired—expired like a carton of milk with an old expiration date.

Even when I sat on the edge of the bed holding Courtney as we contacted our parents, I knew that God, the same God that raised Lazarus from the dead, was not a respecter of persons; therefore, I was good. There was no way God could misinterpret this message. I was a mother who not only cared for my own children, but also for other children whose mothers needed assistance. If my servant heart and sacrificing spirit did not count, then why was I serving God? The tangible evidence before me led me to believe that Michela would wake up! I just knew it!

Although there were many, my first outward expression of anger was the night Michela did not awake from her heavenly sleep. When she did not get up. I sat there in the ER, holding my Bible, moving from shock to denial, and then boom! I ran outside of Arlington Memorial Hospital and began to take all my anger out on a tree that just happened to be close by. I now see more clearly that even that tree, which is still there today, was part of the Father's purpose. As I pounded and screamed at that tree, it was like proclaiming, "Okay. I am angry. Now. Will you please listen?" Because things were not going as I planned. I got mad. I was so mad I refused to pray with the ministers who came to the house offering their condolences. I just stood in shock, denying that my God who is supposed to supply all my needs could injure me so badly. This type of pain is unimaginable. I did not even know there was pain this deep. And anyone, including God, who would inflict such a blow had to be my enemy.

I tell you about this not to make excuses for my behavior. In my right mind, this would never occur, mostly because I was raised to have a respectful fear of God. Before Michela's passing over, I possessed a healthy awareness of and appreciation for the dangers which accompany cursing God. But your grieving loved one's mind is struggling to make sense of the senseless. Therefore, it is important to allow rational or logical explanations to temporarily co-inhabit with the irrational and illogical. We observe, support, and allow the Holy Spirit to have His perfect way with anger. I cannot even remember how many years it was before I realized, as Job said, "Though He slay me, yet will I trust Him" (Job 13:15a, NKJV). But I can tell you this: it did not happen soon. Even today, the words are hard to repeat. They are difficult because, just like your grieving loved one, I understand what "slay" really means. Nevertheless, in God's perfect timing, trust did return, and stronger than ever. This was mainly because I realized very quickly that living without Him was not an option for me at all, so I decided to instead be angry in silence. I would go into these rages and scream at the top of my lungs at God into a towel or in the shower. I would tell Him exactly how I felt over and over again. I would point out people while driving in my car, complete strangers who looked evil or people on the news who were murderers. Even while holding all this in my heart, I continued to go to church, praise, and even teach others about God's love and hope for tomorrow. But truly, it was a kind of numbing, rehearsed, publicly accepted response. I said the right things and responded correctly. I said Amen at the right time. I shouted Hallelujah at the right time. But, in my heart, I no longer trusted God.

When Michela passed over, I was a first year graduate student at UT Southwestern Medical in Dallas, Texas. As a first year physical therapy student, it was one of the most exciting times in my life. Our entire family had sacrificed immensely over the last six years for me to be there, and now it was here. And then God was allowing everything to be turned upside down. It seemed cruel to allow me to get my BA in science, enter and be accepted into one of the most prestigious medical schools in the DFW area, and then take my most precious gift in the world, my child. It felt like the Father was playing games with my understanding, on one side blessing me, while on the other side cursing me.

Sometimes I could almost hear the laughter in my grief-stricken soul. The enemy was using my grief and just enough understanding of the infallible Word of God to entice me away from my ever-present help in a time of trouble (Psalm 46:1). June 2003 started out as one of the happiest times in my life. But just as your grieving loved one will one day attest, sometimes there are no warnings when trials and tribulations come in. By the seventh day of that same month, all previously referenced and trusted realities would be on shaky and unstable ground.

Sharing the Weight of Grief

It was one of the happiest times in our family's life. We had the perfect little family of four—Courtney, the girls, and me. Then God cut me and turned His back on me. I was so confused, sleep deprived, and grief stricken. Most days, it was very easy for the accuser of the brethren to deceive me. You may be experiencing the same with your grieving loved one and their exhausting fight with anger. You must understand, their brain is telling them that, in order to feel better, they have to figure things out. But by now, their understanding is that there is nothing to figure out. This causes a disconnect between the grieving person's conscious mind and reality, placing them in a state where it's like they are trying to connect, but are stuck buffering with no output. The frustrations of not feeling better can cause dis-ease or even more deferment. Remember, deferred hope makes the heart sick.

The great news is that the Holy Spirit held on to me tightly, not allowing me to be consumed by shock, denial, or anger. Anger can exhibit itself in many different ways: through frustration, pride, selfishness, or stubbornness about listening to reason. It is okay. Just remember to continue to implement the **Principles**. Your grieving loved one's wounded, hope-deferred heart is a precious treasure. Questions of the heart can only be adequately addressed by the Holy Spirit. He will bring them out in His timing. Only He can reframe, revise, and realign them completely and successfully.

Of course, my angry heart did not make it easy for those attempting to support me. If they were a widower or widow, I would ask how anyone could compare the death of a grown, married woman or man with that of an innocent child. If the supporter child passed over, I would in my soul silently search out differences, such as if the child was stillborn, or younger or older than Michela. I placed a lot of energy during this time keeping myself isolated. I would sometimes even rationalize no one could understand because they did not birth Michela. This included Courtney.

To an uninformed supporter or observer, these thoughts and actions might seem destructive. Hopefully, you have by now come to understand that during times of grief, the lines of good and evil can become somewhat blurred. We do know that the Father is omnipresent and omniscient, and He reigns over the just and the unjust. The Father allows emotions and feelings. He allowed my heart to be in shock, denial, and, yes, even anger. He treated me as though I was still an uninformed sinner, or even better, as though I was a little infant unable to see the dangers around me as I kicked and screamed to have my own way. Yes, allowing anger to remain unchecked for too long can be detrimental. However, the mighty Comforter is located right on the scene. God had not forsaken me. God had not abandoned me or turned a deaf ear to my cries that night in Arlington Memorial Hospital ER.

During periods of anger, a grieving person may be angry at themselves for the way they handled or are dealing with their grief. Like me, they might question their own actions, wondering things like whether we should have even gone swimming, or whether being distracted with medical school caused me to miss obvious signs. Anger is an equal opportunist, allowing the grieving heart to easily move from self-directed anger to anger directed at God and others. Your grieving loved one might be angry at God for not saving their loved one, or not intervening to stop or derail the plans of someone or something. It is even not uncommon for anger to be directed at the person who passed over, especially in cases of suicide or if there were contributing mental conditions. If we stop and think rationally, we would all agree that these feelings of deflected anger usually are very irrational, and often do not make sense. But, nonetheless, anger is a very real emotion. It is also an emotion that can be addressed and taken captive.

Several years ago, Courtney shared something with me around one of our grief milestones. He told me while working on June 7 (Michela's passing over date), he began to experience anxiety as the hour of her passing approached. He said he could feel the nervous energy begin to slowly turn into anger. He said, "Jacqueline, I could feel the anger growing inside of me. I did not know why, but even the sounds of people's footsteps made me anxious and then angry. I remember thinking how happy she"—a female coworker clicking her heels—"sounded and wishing she would go away." He said he listened in anger pretty much all day. Previously, Courtney had always taken the day off on Michela's passing over day, but that particular year he had decided to work. Whether or not to take a day off is completely a personal decision made by your grieving loved one based on how they feel at any point. Courtney decided on his own to work on the 2018 anniversary date of Michela's passing. I really do not remember him discussing it with me at all until the night before, which was a bit odd, but by that point in our grief journey together we had mastered giving each other grieving space. It seemed like a good idea to me, because I typically never take the day off. And, although it was emotionally hard for Courtney, he made it.

As the supporter, you must understand that this could have gone many different ways. Courtney could have changed his mind before or at any point during the day. As the supporter, especially during the early days, months, and years, your only concern is the griever. This is why it is very important to have an intimate relationship with your grieving loved one and to remember anniversary dates. Our supporters would organize their schedules to ensure we were completely covered. I encourage you to write the date down and be intentional about remembering it. Try your best to remember other trigger dates and periods. You will come to learn your grieving loved one's patterns and emotional struggles. Most will be related to seasonal events and anniversaries, such as passing over dates, birth dates, holidays, and milestones of siblings, family, and friends. These periods are not concrete and can last days, weeks, or even months before or after the event or anniversary. Therefore, there is no heavenly way you can provide the intimate care your griever will need whenever it is needed. The need for comfort might come in the morning, in the middle of the day, or late at night. It might come all at once, like a flood, or in little bite-sized episodes. Sometimes for me it would come during Michela's favorite commercial, or at midnight because I was awakened from my sleep. Trust me, the scenarios are limitless and can last for years. In order to be committed and available for the long haul, you must become an expert at casting and implementing the **Principles**. Quietly observe to ensure your prayers and supplications do not require professional intervention. If no professional intervention is required, we continue positioning ourselves to intercede, not intervene.

As you pray for your grieving loved one's heart to be released from the snare of anger, you will begin to witness changes. My most helpful supporters would listen to my nonsense, allowing me to get it out. They never attempted, unless led by the Holy Spirit, to correct me. They understood and had faith in the truth. The Word teaches us that light and darkness cannot inhabit the same space. My heart was a very dark place for some time, but John 1:5 (NIV) proclaims that "the light shines in the darkness, and the darkness has not overcome it." This scripture proclaims victory over your grieving loved one's heart. Because Jesus has already done the work and returned, now the Holy Spirit is indwelling, inside and with us. This is truth we can trust. Neither evil nor anger can forever inhabit the heart that God has already accepted as His. We stand interceding because a soul that is burdened down with overwhelming grief feels like all hope is deferred. They are unable to rationally move between their sick heart and confused mind. Your grieving loved one's brain and emotions are overstimulated. I can remember telling a close friend at Michela's home-going celebration to please not allow anyone to touch me. I felt like a balloon filled with water bouncing over hot coals. Nevertheless, the Father came and found me. His Word teaches us that even if we made our beds in hell, even there he would find us (Psalm 139:8). If we believe this to be true—and I am living testimony that it is so—we can trust this truth to lead your grieving loved one safely to and through these shadows of darkness. Although I knew I would never make it, and that the grief of Michela passing over would kill me, it did not, and now the anger has gone. Now, when thoughts come—and they do still come—I receive them. Then, I take captive every negative thought that comes against life. Although the amount of captured negative thoughts has lessened since 2003 and I'm no longer consumed, the enemy will probably always attempt to use them to distract and/or hinder the Father's plans for me. I use the word *attempt* because of Jeremiah 29:11 and Psalm 37:4.

I have come to an understanding, through my anger, of the truth for me in regards to Jeremiah 29:11 and Psalm 37:4. Jeremiah 29:11 (KJV) says, "For I know the thoughts that I think toward you, saith the Lord, thoughts of peace, and not of evil, to give you an expected end." Remember, I was upset, because how could God not define this as harm or evil? But after a series of close calls (escaping several bad automobile accidents in early 2004), God showed me His sovereignty—just as, in due time, Jehovah-Roi, our protector will guide and reveal things directly into the mind and heart of your grieving loved one. The Master Comforter reminded me that Michela never belonged to me. He did this by guiding me to Michela's Bible. It was a day during which I had been upset about Michela passing over without me there. In my mind, it just did not seem right. She was alone without me in her time of trouble. Then, deep in my soul, I heard so clearly: "Read her Bible." I opened it and the pages immediately separated at Revelation 4, "The Throne in Heaven." Michela had highlighted these words and placed two stars, one at each corner:

> *After this I looked, and there before me was a door standing open in heaven. And the voice I had first heard speaking to me like a trumpet said, "Come up here, and I will show you what must take place after this." At once I was in the Spirit, and there before*

me was a throne in heaven with someone sitting on it. And the one who sat there had the appearance of jasper and ruby. A rainbow that shone like an emerald encircled the throne. Surrounding the throne were twenty-four other thrones, and seated on them were twenty-four elders. They were dressed in white and had crowns of gold on their heads. From the throne came flashes of lightning, rumblings and peals of thunder. In front of the throne, seven lamps were blazing. These are the seven spirits of God. Also in front of the throne there was what looked like a sea of glass, clear as crystal. In the center, around the throne, were four living creatures, and they were covered with eyes, in front and in back. The first living creature was like a lion, the second was like an ox, the third had a face like a man, the fourth was like a flying eagle. Each of the four living creatures had six wings and was covered with eyes all around, even under its wings. Day and night they never stop saying:

> *"Holy, holy, holy*
> *is the Lord God Almighty,*
> *who was, and is, and is to come."*
> *(Revelation 4:1–8, NIV)*

It was like my heart and mind immediately came into agreement with the Word of God. Who would have known? I know, God did. But I would never have imagined that God would use Michela to minister to her own grieving mother's heart. The scriptures began to open up to me in a different way, and my anger got better and better. As I have come to realize, life and death are personal. Michela had already been communing with the Father concerning what would come next. She was saved and knew her Father's voice. I could hear the Holy Spirit gently applauding my service as a goodly, obedient, earthly parent for completing our most important job in the lives of our earthly children—teaching them the Father's voice. Of course, as any master teacher, the Holy Spirit wasted no time and immediately revealed other areas of doubt and uncertainty within my heart, scriptures I had been struggling with since being dropped on this overwhelming journey of grief. Scriptures such as Psalm 37:4, which says, "Delight thyself also in the Lord; and He shall give thee the desires of thine heart." I just knew there was absolutely no way God would be able to explain this one away. I was a cynic, almost taunting God. I am sharing this very disrespecting season in my life to allow you to see just how gentle and easy God was with my brokenness. He allowed me to question Him for a season. He allowed me to deny and doubt Him for a season. He guided me out and to Him through His Word and the leading of the Holy Spirit in His due season. "I also pray that you will understand the incredible greatness of God's power for us who believe him. This is the same mighty power that raised Christ from the dead and seated him in the place of honor at God's right hand in the heavenly realms" (Ephesians 1:19–20, NLT).

The Holy Spirit spent hours softly speaking and revealing to me, "Jacqueline, Michela delights in Me, and you will one day again delight in Me. Yes, you have My Word in you, and yes, you brought Michela to Me and placed her in an atmosphere where she learned of Me and loved Me. I am a good parent, better than you could ever be. Just as you had no idea Michela had communed with Me about what she would experience on June 7, 2003, you have no idea of your heart or its desires."

Over many months, the Holy Spirit continued to reveal new things to me. Even today, I still do not completely understand everything He has entrusted into my heart. But I have come to trust the truth regardless of my limited understanding. The truth is as your grieving loved one moves along this journey, they will come to understand, just as good earthly parents show gratitude toward their goodly children, God searches His children's minds and hearts, as He desires us to align ourselves with His will. My desire to have Michela here in the physical could have never overridden Michela's desire to be with her Heavenly Father.

It was many years between my revelation about Jeremiah 29:11 and Psalm 37:4. As I look back now, it was all strategically positioned through the watchful hands of a loving Father. The Father I had called cruel, absent, and cold. The Father whom, in my grief, I had refused to pray to or acknowledge. Yet He waited on me and was patient with me, just as He will pursue, wait for, and be patient with your angry, grieving loved one. There is nothing your grieving loved one can say that the Father has not already heard and did not already know they would say at this season of their journey. As the supporters, we become masters at the implementation of the **Principles** as we quietly observe to ensure our prayers and supplications do not require additional professional assistance. If no professional intervention is required, we continue our posture of interceding and not intervening.

Anger over the loss of a loved one can take many different forms. This is why it is important to have a close, intimate relationship with your grieving loved one. In the year of the sixteenth anniversary of Michela's passing over, we faced an additional challenge: the first anniversary of Courtney's mother's passing. Approximately three or four days before June 7, 2019, Courtney began to look worried. I would ask him, "Is something wrong?" He would reply no. Over the next few days, he became even more irritated, but continued to insist nothing was wrong. I immediately began to pray, mainly because he was really beginning to irritate me. While praying one morning, the Holy Spirit reminded me that this year would be different for Courtney because of the passing over of his mother. I had completely disengaged and had somehow forgotten the close proximity of their passing. It is amazing how just going to the Father in prayer provides quick guidance and confidence in our times of shock, denial, and/or anger. As 1 John 5:14 (NIV) tells us, "This is the confidence we have in approaching God: that if we ask anything according to His will, He hears us." Courtney, on the other hand, had no clue he was angry and continued with his established June 7 rituals: he goes to work, and then afterward he drives to the grave site to place flowers on Michela's headstone. We made it to and through the day, but Courtney's anger continued. I continued to pray, as well as do little things to make his day easier, such as taking the trash out and folding his laundry (as Veterans can be really particular about their laundry). I also purchased a new shoe rack, as he was complaining about having too many shoes lying around. It is the little things you do that will gently assist the Father in bringing your grieving loved one back to gratitude. Gratitude is a great tool to use against anger, because it can be applied in the most subtle ways.

Courtney loves to date me. After thirty-three years of marriage, we are both so grateful to be together and in love. And finally, our tradition of dating is what led to a breakthrough with Courtney's anger. At one of our usual locations, the Comedy Club, we were spotlighted as semi-celebrities when the host asked who had been married the longest. Our (at the time) thirty-one-plus years was enough to get us cheers and claps from everyone in the audience. Just like that, the heaviness of anger lifted from Courtney's face. When we returned home, we sat outside on our patio, enjoying the unusually nice evening, and Courtney began to pour out his journey over the last few weeks. He started with, "I do not know why I have been so angry, but everything was getting under my skin. Even the sounds of my co-workers footsteps coming toward me would make me upset." He believed it was because he had underestimated year sixteen without Michela. It was not until he began to explain how he had been feeling over the course of the last several days that we made the unsettling connection. It was not just year sixteen of life without Michela. It was also the first Courtney had to travel this journey without his mother. He simply underestimated the extra weight associated with the first year without Michela and his mother. As mentioned before, the "firsts" are usually more difficult because they come without reference.

Although he believed he was good after our moonlight conversation, he remained in the trenches until a few days after his mother's passing over date came and went. My position throughout all of this was to implement the principles within this book. I also learned that with some relationships, we have to consciously plant seeds of forgiveness and gratitude. I had to remember to quickly let things go and to be willing to apologize first. In our house, we have termed this "taking one for the team." We think of it in this way because it means we are sacrificing for the good of all. It does no one any good to fight with anger, especially anger rooted in loss, because even if you win, the team loses. The Word of God states that "the anger of man does not produce the righteousness of God" (James 1:20, ESV). And trust me, I tried and tested anger; it is the most exhausting and spiritually draining phase or stage of grief for most believers. We are created to thrive in love and life. This is God's will and plan for all His children.

It is important to trust the truth and lean not to your own understanding. Pray and ask the Father to help your grieving loved one have the strength to release their anger and forgive. Use Jesus' last prayer to the Father, as He prayed for those who knew not what they were doing when they nailed Him to the cross. Your grieving loved one, like Courtney, might not be able to see the cloud of anger he or she is experiencing until the anniversary date has come and gone. This is success. Just as Courtney was able to conquer his day and stay at work. Each victory, no matter how small or seemingly insignificant, is one step closer to reality and truth. This awareness brings us to the next transitional blend, which is a very important one.

Transitory Blending Phase

We have discussed shock, denial, and now anger. Please understand that phases can last for seconds, minutes, hours, days, weeks, and even years. This is why it is important to remember the first three principles. Sharpen **Principle 1**. Read and study your Word. Read scriptures about the character of God. Join a Bible study class. Share your journey confidentially with others you trust. Remember, it only takes one misrepresented statement to crumble months of trust. During this time, **Principle 2** and **Principle 3** are extremely important. I had totally missed what was going on with Courtney, but through prayer and supplication, the Holy Spirit led me straight to quietness and the Comedy Club, where we simply laughed and were celebrated, which fostered an atmosphere of gratitude for us both. Even though Courtney and I have seen more years together than apart, only God knows the heart of man, and we must be very careful not to judge or condemn. Through observation and intimacy, we can assess and assist, intercede, based on what we know to be truth. We can trust that the Father will send all the help you need to support and comfort His broken-hearted child. Your grieving loved one will say things like, "I feel like I'm going crazy," or "I feel numb." It is my humble opinion that these words occur most often during times of transitory blending, when it is most difficult to place emotions in one neat category, when the next emotion comes before the last emotion has been taken captive. It is during these times that you the supporter must die to self, when the will of the Father is more important even than maintaining your earthly fellowship with the person you have committed to help.

One of my supporters would gently remind me to "get over myself." It stung like crazy the first time. And I can remember my first response being "What does she know?" Now, eighteen years down this journey, we have come to use it as shorthand whenever our flesh does not want to align according to the Word of God. We usually allow each other to vent, cry, or curse—yes, we do have our moments—and then the sound-minded one in the situation proclaims God's glory and acknowledges Him as Lord by making the sound and wise statement: "get over yourself." We usually laugh and move on. Words like this must be said under the strict guidance of the Holy Spirit. Always remember your words are like a two-edged sword that can cut and injure those around us. If cutting is to be done, and sometimes it must, it should only occur after praying to the Holy Spirit for discernment. When my supporter was led by the Holy Spirit to remind me to "get over myself," those words were extremely hard for her. She is most comfortable within a "gentle as a dove" role. Nevertheless, when God requires you to move in a specific way, you must trust His plan and not your own, even if it pushes you toward new things, words, or actions. Remember, God is working things out for the good of all. This includes you. Your life and walk with God will be renewed after this journey, as well. Now, when my supporter and I look back and ponder over how God was working in the background, we realize that He was speaking to both of us in different ways on the same subject. He was positioning her lips to speak while softening my heart to receive.

I cannot over-express the need to not grieve the Holy Spirit, nor to stop His movement. If I could insert highlights and stars here, like Michela placed in her Bible for me, or red italics as when Jesus speaks in the New

Testament, I would. Your constant communication with the Holy Spirit is extremely essential. Revise the following prayer and make it your own, then pray it often:

"Father, allow Your voice to be the loudest voice in my day. Give me ears to hear and the courage and strength to obey quickly, trusting in Your thoughts and ways and not my own. In Jesus' Holy Name, Amen.

Follow this truth and in no time you will be a master at yielding to the Spirit, a servant on meat, as it says in Hebrews 5:12–14. You must daily examine your heart's motives, acknowledge that you are only a vessel, and allow yourself to learn from the Holy Spirit. You must also be self-forgiving and confident. Will you have moments of uncertainty? Yes. Nevertheless, the Father will always be there to tell you that it's okay. Keep this book handy. Whenever uncertainty or doubt arises, go to the **Quick Reference Guide**, select whatever season you are led to refresh yourself on, and go back to the basics. This is what maturing in the Word feels like. Regardless of what or how you feel, your first response should always be: "What does the Word say?" Simply go back to your **Principles**. This type of service requires you to be in constant fellowship with the Master Teacher. Remember to follow the **Principles** with a spirit of servitude. In the words of my wisdom-rich grandmother, Mrs. Carrie Agnew, don't go around wearing your feelings on your sleeve. She didn't coin the phrase, but she sure knew how to master her feelings and emotions. So take your heart off of your sleeve and get over yourself as often as you need. Just like Simon of Cyrene, you are only sharing the weighty cross. This is not your journey. Therefore, during times of frustration, fear, or anger, forgive quickly and speak words of gratitude as much as possible. This season will soon pass.

CHAPTER 4

Guilt

Most guilt, as mine did, develops out of the grieving person's inability to keep their loved one alive. Our rational selves tell us this makes no sense. However, to your grieving loved one's current position on their journey, this might seem to be the case. My mind carried my burdened heart back and forth, moving between 2003 and 1993. I would stay up pondering it, trying to decide when my fatal errors were made. Was it when I decided to move to Texas, with its troublesome air quality, from the Bay Area? If only I had not suggested we move to Texas from where the air quality is so pure. Then, back to 2003, I would think, if only I had stayed home instead of returning back to the water park after taking Michela home to Courtney. If only I had not been preoccupied with PT school and was more focused on Michela's asthma. I carried around amazing guilt, and most of it was self-directed. I did not need any outside help. Just as your grieving loved one might, I said untrue and horrible things about myself in the quietness of my heart and mind. I would exhaust myself attempting to play back the entire day, searching for where I went wrong. Should I blame the pharmacy for giving me the wrong medication? This error meant another trip to the pharmacy. Maybe if she had gotten the medication earlier, the spasm would not have consumed her lungs. Your grieving loved one might have self-directed guilt at the same time as they are experiencing anger at themselves or others. The guilt may also accompany being angry at the person who has passed over. How could they have committed suicide? Why did they not fight harder to live? Did they not care how much this would hurt those they left behind? In my case, I truly could not understand how or why Michela would choose to be with God instead of with me.

Guilt flows from irrational sources within our imaginations. The Word of God tells us that we need to be "casting down imaginations, and every high thing that exalteth itself against the knowledge of God, and bringing into captivity every thought to the obedience of Christ" (2 Corinthians 10:5, KJV). The truth is that only God controls life and death. This temporarily needed season is the brain's way of throwing things back on the heart, which is actually where we want it to be, strategically positioned in the proximity of our mighty Comforter.

On most days I accepted God's sovereign will for that day. But there were days, and still are, when I had to control those blaming thoughts. Just as all the stages and phases of grief are unique, so are the many factors surrounding the depth or duration of guilt. These may include things such as the circumstances surrounding the loss or the relationship between your grieving loved one and the person who has passed over. Even family dynamics can make things different, either more or less complicated. But regardless of the relationship, family dynamics, or circumstances surrounding the loss, God's thoughts and plans are expected and will not harm us.

As the supporter, it is important for you to understand that during grief-related guilt, it may become difficult to distinguish between our emotions and God's unchanging Word. This may be your grieving loved one's position. Courtney and I are the oldest children in both of our families. Neither of us have sisters. Because I am the oldest of five, all boys, being responsible for others came naturally to me. When I became a mother, it was like, "Yes! This is something I can be great at—something I have been training for since the birth of my youngest brother when I was a teenager." I had a reference for all of it, which gave me confidence, vision, and determination; humans respond well to having references. But grief, especially guilt-stricken grief, operates within its own set of unknowns, even if the loss was known to be coming, such as after a long battle with cancer. You must remember that God never designed our hearts and minds to deal with or understand death or loss. We were designed to live in a wonderful, eternal, free-of-loss garden. Unfortunately, due to sin, death has found and will find its way to all mankind.

I can remember crying out "she needed me, and I was not there!" so much my throat ached. I can remember the looks I would get sometimes. And many times for good reason. Many of those concerned stares came from mature believers who felt their suffering provided me comfort. But suffering is not a prerequisite for being a grief support. The first and most important trait would be learning to trust and lean only on God's infallible truths, which will strengthen as you practice boldly speaking God's Word over all emotions, circumstances, and self-doubt. The only prerequisite is your desire to seek Father with your whole heart.

Guilt is very exhausting and drains the body. I would wake up in guilt, conduct my day in guilt, and then lie my head down to go to sleep at night in guilt. This much pain had to have a cause. It was too much pain not to have a source or root cause. Denial didn't help. Anger didn't help. So, something or someone had to be the source. And if it wasn't God or Michela, it must be *me*. In my despair and overstimulated, sleep-deprived mind, it was me. I had neglected my child at her most needy hour. I was the one who missed the signs and symptoms and allowed my daughter to be outside playing during a Texas ozone alert. In Texas, the local news provides daily ozone alerts to assist those who struggle with breathing impairments. It was our normal routine to check those before planning our days. But that day, I had to study for a huge anatomy and physiology exam with our group's cadaver. I was so overwhelmed about making the correct cuts, making incisions and isolating the correct structures, and being careful not to damage nerves and vessels we would need later, that there was no room for the news or ozone reports. Thus, no matter how hard my family and friends tried to convince me otherwise, in my mind, the only answer for this type of pain was *me*. I continued this way of thinking until one day the Holy Spirit showed me through a series of dreams that Michela chose, as her Bible had given testimony, to be with God.

Your grieving loved one's mind is grief-stricken and exhausted, which gives way to strange and sometimes strategically positioned dreams. These dreams might even offer your grieving loved one mustard seed-sized glimpses of potential hope. In one profound dream that I will never forget, I was moaning and crying out in inconsolable, grief-stricken anguish, "You need me," when this huge, very strong, almost soothing Presence touched my soul. My words changed while I was speaking them. The words were so close to pouring out that I could already hear them. But instead, I said "I need you." My words were realigned and immediately changed. God took my words in mid-air and then gave me ears to hear. It was *not* Michela who was in need, but rather *me*.

Guilt has no home within the rational thought processes of a sound mind. Sound minds have been granted to us through the Word of God, "for God hath not given us a spirit of fear; but of power, and of love, and of a sound mind" (2 Timothy 1:7, KJV). Guilt hinders or cancels out the good reports and lovely thoughts that we are instructed to be meditating on in our hearts and minds (Philippians 4:8). This is what guilt does, and what it might be doing in the heart of your grieving loved one. This is the reason it is important for you to never cease from praying. You will hear things which you know are simply not true. These may be statements such as, "I was the cause of my mother's death, because we got into a huge agreement the day before," or, "If I had picked up the groceries instead of my husband, he would not have been in that fatal accident." As the supporter, it is best to just silently pray during these times. Practice encouraging them through nonverbal cues such as nodding your head, taking their hand, or caressing their back as you allow your grieving loved one to say their own words out loud. Eventually, the Holy Spirit, who never leaves your grieving loved one's side, will begin to fill all deficits in their heart.

Most of my guilt was related to the days leading up to Michela's passing over. I was the expert—and no one except the Holy Spirit could straighten those crooked roads. I believed that my thoughts and understanding were superior to that of God's Word, my therapist, and any other person who would dare to challenge my relationship with my grief-related guilt. Now, with so many years to reference, I can look back on those days and see how exhausting and isolated my guilt-centered perspective had become. The same God, the author and finisher of our faith (Hebrews 12:2), confirms our desire to look toward Jesus. He and only He has been seated at the right hand of God. Therefore, we must trust even more in **Principle 1**: "The work belongs to God." You have to trust the truth. God's Word refused to allow me to be paralyzed by shock, bombarded with the unanswered questionings of denial, or overwhelmed with anger. Our Heavenly Father, in His omnipresent, omnipotent, and omniscient character, has not been taken by surprise. He is fully aware of all high things, including my misguided need to blame myself and others. He is here. He has not forsaken us. You can trust that He will bring beauty and the garment of praise in its due season. Until then, we apply our principles and trust the truth, "and we know that for those who love God all things work together for good, for those who are called according to His purpose" (Romans 8:28, ESV).

Transitory Blending Phase

After coming to the realization that God was not going to change His mind that night at the Arlington Memorial Hospital, it was very easy for me to be overcome with anger. I believe that this anger, or fighting this anger, guided me into the next stage or phase of my journey. Fighting God's unmoved Word takes a lot out of His children. I am reminded of Acts 9:5b (KJV), when the Lord told Saul that "it is hard for thee to kick against the pricks." Wow, I'm living testimony. God's will and desire won't yield to shock, denial, anger, or guilt—or my need to have answers. Despite having minutes, hours, days, and months over the last eighteen years in which I frequented guilt—insisting that something this bad does not "just happen," that pain like this has to have an origin, and that origin was with me—eventually, all guilt-stricken conversation will have to stand before the infallible Word of God. As the supporter, you must understand that this process may be slow and zigzagging. But the Holy Spirit is there, waiting, conversing to your grieving loved one's current heart condition.

My journals do not provide an exact timeframe for this stage or phase; what I do know is that, like the blind man in John 9, I was once blind, but now I can see. Now, seeing clearer, I acknowledge the fact that God was with me the entire time, from His decision to call Michela home to His choice of who would be with her when she crossed over. I understand that my guilt, along with my shock, anger, and denial, was not normal for a non-grieving person. It was instead my mind's attempt to understand and respond to the perception that I had somehow failed in my duties and obligations as a mother, or that I had done something wrong by moving to a state with such a bad climate when Michela was two years old. My exhausted mind would generate a jumbled mixture of feelings, including doubt, shame, inadequacy, insecurity, failure, unworthiness, self-judgment, blame, anxiety, and fear. Some moments I felt them all at the same time. Some days I would spend hours trying to convince myself that I was in control at the same time as these emotional blends would be swirling through my mind and heart. I would say things like, "It doesn't matter how I feel; she's still gone," as a kind of passive-aggressive way to be self-condemning and angry. This is exactly what your grieving loved one will experience.

Times of transition are hard, but critically necessary to isolate temporarily permissible thoughts and ways of a hope-deferred, sick heart. It is God who identifies and isolates these high imagination things that need to be taken captive. It is the Holy Spirit who can speak directly and precisely into the soul. "Likewise the Spirit also helpeth our infirmities: for we know not what we should pray for as we ought: but the Spirit itself maketh intercession for us with groanings which cannot be uttered. And he that searcheth the hearts knoweth what is the mind of the Spirit, because he maketh intercession for the saints according to the will of God" (Romans 8:26–27, KJV).

We position ourselves to follow our principles, allowing God to do the work as we prayerfully and quietly intercede, allowing the mighty Comforter to make intercessions for your grieving loved one. We are not perplexed by the appearance of doubt, shame, inadequacy, insecurity, failure, worthlessness, self-judgment, blame, anxiety, or fear which may or may not come. We are confident and trust the truth: "Blessed are those who mourn, for they shall be comforted" (Matthew 5:4, ESV).

CHAPTER 5

Depression

Sorrow and depression are probably the most widely accepted stages or phases of grief, especially within the body of Christ. This is because most people associate depression immediately with grief. As your grieving loved one starts showing less signs of shock, denial, anger, and guilt, they may seem to be coping and dealing with life better. But this uproots deep, previously quieted sorrow and provides the tangible evidence that your grieving loved one is present—and it is in being present with our emotions that the emptiness from the loss and reality surfaces or resurfaces. Although the enemy can and will use depression, depression can also result due to the emotional and physical demands of grieving on the body.

Chemicals that keep our brain functioning can become depleted during times of stress. Depression is the result of a chemical depletion and is a legitimate medical problem—not a spiritual battle to conquer. Your grieving loved one will probably experience and routinely visit moments of overwhelming sorrow. They may exhibit feelings of emptiness, despair, deep loneliness, and/or yearning for their loved one who has passed. Sorrow and depression are natural and temporary emotions involved in the coping with, and eventual acceptance of, traumatic events and circumstances.

Although my soul was sorrowful from the moment my grief journey began, the subtler and less-apparent demands of sorrow had been overshadowed by the more boisterous stages and phases—shock, denial, anger, and guilt. As your grieving loved one begins to deal more successfully and completely in areas related to the loss, open wounds will begin to surface surrounding their heart. The Word teaches us to expect sorrow and mourning to flee away as we await gladness and joy (Isaiah 51:11b). For now, it is important for you to remember that at this point of their journey, their sickly, hope-deferred heart cannot withstand words like *gladness* and *joy*. For now, imagine seeing everything in black and white. I truly felt as though all the color had been zapped away from my life. Everything, and I mean *everything*, was clouded by my grief perspective, including the Word of God.

I have always been a diligent biblical scholar, but it was no longer applying to the thoughts and desires of my mind and heart. Yes, I loved God. But in His silence, it was easy to wonder and even sometimes slip back into questioning how this type of pain could come from such a loving God. The words of Job, "Though He slay me, yet will I trust in Him" (Job 13:15a, KJV), were still just hollow words. But it was exactly where the Holy Spirit would be working next in His master plan to heal my wounded and broken heart. The Holy Spirit began teaching me, saying "Yes, the same God." These conversations would resonate throughout my day. While brushing my hair or teeth, I would hear the Holy Spirit standing up in my heart—"Yes, the same God." When anniversary dates and birthdays would come—"Yes, the same God." When things would go good or bad, the overwhelming theme in my heart, placed there by the Holy Spirit, would always be the same. "Yes, the same God." He wanted to provide me with daily, undeniable evidence presented in a way I could understand, teaching me as He taught David and Job. As 1 Chronicles 29:14b (NLT) tells us, "Everything we have has come from You, and we give You only what You first gave us!" No amount of bargaining (which is sometimes considered a phase or stage of grief) will remove those who love the Lord and seek His will for their lives from this very important truth.

It was this truth which made my heart sorrowful: the same God who loves me is the same God who is allowing this pain to come to me. My soul was so void of hope. But by this point of my grief journey, I had mastered keeping things quiet. I had learned to say the right things. I was great at washing the ashes from my face to keep up the good fight of faith appearance. The last thing any spirit-filled, choir-singing, door-ushering, speaking in tongues Christian would want is for anyone to find out how sorrowful they truly are when no one is watching. I think this is why isolation becomes so common during depression: keeping up appearances takes more energy than just drifting into the background. But because of this desire to keep up appearances, your grieving loved one's panic-stricken midnight calls might not align with their Sunday going-to-church spiritual presentations.

Looking back, I can see how privately withdrawn my life had become. Most days, I felt numb and foggy. The so-called normal things of life, like brushing my teeth, eating, and, yes, even getting out of bed were too overwhelming for me to face. Remember our earlier conversation on signs and symptoms of complicated grief, such as focusing on little else but the loved one's death? It is not okay for your grieving loved one to remain in a state of persistent longing or pining for the deceased. These types of signs should be addressed immediately by the family, and if warranted, or even just as an agreed-upon precautionary step, reach out to a professional grief counselor. Courtney, Erica, and I have done this on many occasions: we have come to believe this was our family's game changer leading to longevity with joy. It's not just making it to 2021 (Hallelujah post COVID); it's also living a full, functional life anticipating love, peace, and hope. So, if you ever feel a need to seek help, please do not second-guess your heart.

If you are still reading this book, your heart will know if your grieving loved one needs additional assistance.

The type of depression you are capable of overseeing from afar does not involve habitual thoughts of life holding no meaning or chronic self-loathing. We encourage you to be a silent observer, understanding that some signs of depression will include feelings of not wanting to be around others or of being guarded. This is completely temporarily permissible. As the supporter, you need to be fully aware of these feelings and simply allow them. Time has taught me that suppressing or ignoring feelings of sorrow and depression only intensifies the waves of grief. Waves of grief will come. During the first days, weeks, months, and sometimes years, your grieving loved one will feel like their emotions are on a pendulum. Again, this is common and nothing to be alarmed about. When questions based in depression or deep sorrow arise, such as "Why did God allow my mother to get COVID," "When will I stop crying," or "Why is God doing this to me," allow silence to come and have its perfect way. Go back to your nonverbal communication we previously discussed. As they make their pleas, try making intentional deep diaphragm breaths. Allow them to pour out as much sorrow as they can. Posture your body as humbly as you know how. Some grievers welcome hugs; others would rather receive a gentle touch on their arm or shoulder. The only cure for a believer who is heartsick is the Word of God—which is sometimes the very thing that believers cannot bring themselves to reopen. You need to be confident in whom you trust, knowing these times will get lighter.

Extreme sorrow and depression are not the traits given to us from a good good Father. Hopelessness will recede to the infinite character of our Almighty God.

My journey with sorrow was depleting. It was so draining. Inwardly I felt weighted down and overused while outwardly I was focused, on point, and doing the thing. Inwardly I was screaming "Can anyone hear me?" at the top of my lungs while outwardly I was smiling and saying, "Have a great day, ain't God good." The masquerade makes talking with and being around people difficult because it brings up feelings of hopelessness. "Why can't I just get over this?" "What's wrong with me?" "I'm the only one still dealing with this loss." These types of words are common during times of sorrow and depression. You might hear statements like "What's the point of going on?" or "Sometimes I just wish I would have died, too." Being fully aware that suicidal thoughts and conversation must always be carefully weighed and assessed, it is during this time that your intimacy with your grieving loved one will count the most. Assess their words and actions, and their ability to carry any actions through. If at any time you feel the need to contact a grief professional, or even 911, do so. You are encouraged to always prayerfully follow the leading of the Holy Spirit. Sometimes just confidentially sharing your thoughts with someone trained as a grief facilitator (such as you will find at a Grief Hotline) can be very effectual.

Grief, sadness, and depression are temporarily permissible to soothe the griever's broken heart. The Word of God teaches us that "hope deferred makes the heart sick" (Proverbs 13:12a, NIV). Just as with your grieving loved one's lonely heart, my heart was so troubled with the weight of life without Michela. My hopes and dreams for her education, the children she would have, and the life she should have and would have lived were taken away. Most of my sorrow came from having my hope so violently snatched away from me—hope I was sure would *never* return. This is exactly what makes our hearts so sick. Once we have experienced many of the other stages and phases of grief, we face the realization of time, which is still moving forward. To me, it was evident that my life stank and there was nothing anyone could do to make it better. Sorrow became my new normal.

This is also a time when others, such as therapists, doctors, family, and friends, might suggest other forms of help. I can remember refusing to take antidepressants to help me cope. It just did not make sense to my grieving mind. "You want me to take something to make me feel better? How can anything make me feel better?" But there are times when someone might need to be prescribed medication to assist them in coping. Each case must be evaluated independently. As the supporter, your part will be to make sure (as much as possible) that it's being taken as prescribed. This can be done quietly and privately with open-ended questions like, "How are you adjusting to the prescription?" or by asking questions about the intended outcomes, such as, "Is the prescription allowing you to rest more?" Although our desire is to see the grieving loved one leaning on and applying the Word of God, we must remember, just as with Simon, that it is not our journey. God had predestined every step of Jesus' journey, just as He has planned every step of our journeys.

During this season we should use kind and pleasant words to draw the heart close. Pleasant words will render more information, which is what a surrendering, discerning supporter is looking for. Our ultimate goals during times of sorrow are observation and prayer. We are intimately available so that we may take advantage of opportunities to pray without ceasing for our grieving loved one. They might cry on the phone with you for hours. Allow them to empty themselves completely while you silently pray. It helps me to place my phone on mute. This way, even if I accidently responded too soon, my grieving loved one wouldn't hear me. Then, just when the Holy Spirit leads you, softly ask, "How might we pray, today?" or, "Can we pray?" This is when you pray as you are led by the Spirit. While your loved one was crying on the phone, you were given a front row to their heart. Now, compassionately, just as Jesus did with the Samaritan woman at the well in John 4, you can speak truth over their clouded perspective. Remember **Principle 4**: "The journey belongs to your grieving loved one." Your prayerful position here is to ensure that sorrow and depression does not make their hearts too sick.

God is so loving, He allowed me (for a season) to let my sorrow come first. My grief-stricken heart could not or would not submit to God's sovereign will over Michela's life. While I was lying in the bed, stinking to high heaven, full of guilt, sorrow, and depression, remember it is God who sent Pastor Myers. My God, my heavenly sovereign Father, the One who sat silently as the last breath drifted out of Michela's lungs, is the same God who spoke to my brokenness through the television. For months God had allowed me to lay in bed and pout like a two-year-old, choosing to disengage into my sorrow. I was sorrowful over dates, events, pictures, favorite songs—the list goes on. I would choose to listen to soulful songs like "I Can Only Imagine" by Mercy Me, songs that helped me to set my day in a sorrowful, depression-filled direction. There were times of relief, but they would come later. My initial experiences of sorrow and depression (pre-Pastor Myers) were frequently self-inflicted or -motivated to keep me engulfed in the past with Michela, mostly because my present reality was just too excruciating. The great news is, I'm still here. We made it. Day by day, month by month, and year by year, through the guidance of the Holy Spirit, I unknowingly began to master these principles. My spiritual muscles continued to grow, and had been growing all along. God had not forsaken me. And I had not been consumed. It has been just as the scripture foretold in the first chapter of the book of James. The trying of my faith was beginning to produce things in me that I had absolutely no clue were even there.

I can see more clearly now and have learned my sorrow and depression led my reluctant thoughts and ways to a new approach to surrendering. After I encountered Pastor Myers, it was new and fresh, mainly because I felt I had no other choice. The reality was, I was not getting Michela back in this physical world, and God was not changing His mind. My defiant soul said, "Fine then! Excuse me while I object to this in another way!" The words to the song "I Surrender All" by Mercy Me show exactly what our Heavenly Father is calling us to do. We must surrender shock, denial, anger, and sorrow in order to receive the possibility of a hopeful tomorrow. For me, during those early stages or phases of sorrow and depression, hope hurt. Your grieving loved one's way may be too clouded by their grief perspective, just as I was temporarily convinced that life without hope was safer than being hurt again. If this is true, do not worry, because the Word of God has us completely covered here again. The Word teaches us in John 16:13 that the Holy Spirit is the heart's Intercessor and listens to heavenly conversations on our behalf. This means that even when we are weak and sorrowful from the weight of a deferred or even depleted of hope heart, the Holy Spirit is operating despite our inabilities or weaknesses. Just thinking about this makes me want to praise God, our Heavenly Father, for being such a thoughtful parent and caretaker of our souls. He is an omnipotent and omnipresent Master Creator who placed the Mightiest of the Mighty Comforter right at the source.

During this season, your posture must be one of acknowledgment of God's power over sorrow and depression. As you carefully speak with great expectation words of healing and soundness of mind over your grieving loved one, position yourself with boldness as you proclaim the victory through kind words and gestures of hope. Some examples of gestures you can make include things such as giving them hand-written cards, placing a flower on their car windshield, cutting the grass, or coming over without an invitation, even if it's just to be rejected at the door. Our family was so blessed to have thousands of family and friends to offer us love and support. Supporting the weight of grief is not a spectator sport. You need to be a Simon. You will feel the weight. You will have splinters. You will be exhausted and feel stretched. But you will also be rewarded greatly by your Heavenly Father.

Here are two examples of people who significantly helped us during our grief journey, examples that you may use to inspire your journey of support. The first example is Ron, who has been a close family friend for a good while. Ron's only daughter and Michela had been playmates since they were toddlers. Courtney and Ron were best friends, which made our girls sisters. On occasion, the girls would have sleepovers, so Ron had a close and special relationship with Michela. I know Ron cares for our family and he was devastated about our unexpected tragedy. Now, Ron is not a handyman or lawn expert; he is just a friend with a heart. But to lighten the weight of our grief, he took it upon himself to make our front and back yard neat and tidy for us. It does not seem like much, but it was one of the most relaxing and edifying tokens of love we received during the first few months of our family's grief journey. The smell and look of fresh-cut grass would encourage me to get out of bed and sit outside. Erica and I would play with Elvis, our grief dog, allowing me a brief and needed escape from the demands and strain associated with the early stages of my grief journey. It is hard to deny the glorious wonders of butterflies and birds singing. Sometimes we would hear Ron outside, starting his lawnmower, while other times we would arrive home and find the deed completed. Courtney, Ron or myself, had never discussed this gesture. If Ron had asked our permission, we would have politely turned him down. He never asked us when to come, yet it was always perfectly timed. Our conversations with Ron now have given us clarity. According to him, he never intended to cut our lawn. It's just when he came to comfort us the day after Michela's passing over, his lawnmower, which had just been repaired, had been in his truck. The grass was a little tall, so he cut it. It immediately gave him joy. He said that as he mowed the lawn, he would pray and ask God, why Michela, and why not his daughter? Each time he cut our grass, God would give him more and more understanding and peace. We thought it was all about trying to make us feel better. Little did we know that the Father was once again working things out for the good of all. And while Ron trimmed and manicured our lawn, God was not only allowing him to gently pour into our lives, He was also teaching Ron how to comfort someone without saying a word.

The second person is Hilary. Courtney and Hilary were advertising colleagues. Although I had been introduced to Hilary during company outings and events over the years, most of our family's interactions with Hilary were mainly through her working relationship with Courtney and the girls. Just as Ron supported our family in his own special way, Hilary also found the most thoughtful way to come along beside us on our journey to and through grief. Hilary committed to remembering, which is one of the hardest and most selfless acts of service available to any peripheral supporter. Hilary's commitment to remembering meant that she made her heart revisit Courtney's infirmities each year. Now, it wasn't just that she gave us cards. Our family has received thousands of condolence cards over the past eighteen years, all of which are so very much appreciated. But what's noteworthy about Hilary is that she has shown an unwavering commitment for eighteen years. Hilary has not missed Michela's birthday or passing over anniversary since 2003. She has proven and sealed her faith, love, and hope with tokens of steadfast commitment to stand with us for the long haul. I can remember so many instances of Courtney saying, "Hilary's card came today." For the first five or six years, my grief-centered perspective overclouded Hilary's subtle gestures of love. But now we look forward to seeing Hilary's cards and appreciate the time and effort Hilary has shown us over the years. Hilary's personal commitment to her Heavenly Father to remember our pain combined with His wisdom and grace to be long-suffering. Only God could prescribe exactly what Courtney and I secretly feared the most "forgetting." And yes, she still remembers.

Hilary and Ron's commitment to our family are just two examples of many who have been instrumental in our family's journey to and through grief. It is my hope that you will prayerfully allow the Holy Spirit to guide your decisions and actions as you begin to assist your grieving loved one. It is important to not get distracted or overwhelmed with what to do or what not to do. The Holy Spirit knows exactly what lawns and cards to use; your only work is to apply the **Principles** and trust the truth in steadfast boldness as God does all the work.

Transitory Blending Phase

As time begins to have its perfect way, you will begin to see signs that our Father is working things out for the good for your griever as well as for you. You will see signs that provide evidence of hopeful acceptance, especially for the vigilant eyes of an observing supporter. It won't be the superficial acceptance of "the right thing to say," but rather the acceptance that comes with receiving the fullness of God's sovereignty while surrendering to the acceptance that His plan (even when we don't know what it is or agree) is best for His children. You will begin to witness the following signs. First, you will begin to witness your grieving loved one trusting the truth more. For me, it was trusting the truth that to be absent from the body is to be present with the Lord (2 Corinthians 5:8, KJV). During shock, denial, guilt, anger, and depression, we allow our grief-centered perspective (imaginations and/or high places we have exalted) to have its perfect way in our thoughts and ways. But there will come a time when the Word of God will stand tall against those temporary, permissible crutches, causing your grieving loved one to choose which God they will serve. The Holy Spirit knows exactly where to look and how to call out these mistruths. As this occurs, you will begin to witness outward signs of change in your grieving loved one's journey. When you begin to witness these changes, keep them to yourself. No one could have convinced, charmed, or persuaded me otherwise during my transitory periods. Only the Holy Spirit can arrest the situation right on the scene. Every grieving heart believes they're the best grief expert when it comes to their pain.

I can remember praying once while revisiting anger combined with guilt from an overwhelmed and exhausted hope-deferred heart. I can remember sobbing, praying, and shouting at the top of my lungs. I was upset because I had washed the scent out of one of Michela's undergarments. Yes, I had saved every piece of Michela's dirty clothes. This particular day, a pair of her panties was accidentally washed and cleaned. This sent me on an all-day cry frenzy. How could I have been so stupid? How did they get mixed in with the other clothes? Why does everything have to always be difficult? Can't I at least have her smell? These are the types of things the Father will begin to pry away from your grieving loved one's life. No one knew that I would sit for hours smelling Michela's dirty clothes. No one knew just how physically and emotionally drained I was. And on that day, my emotional fatigue was only enhanced by a trip down "she's really gone" alley. So, I continued this until I began to sorrowfully drift asleep. I can remember feeling almost intoxicated. I felt so exhausted and weighted down. The more I tried to open my eyes, the heavier they became. Until I finally just let go, realizing I couldn't. Studies have identified this sleep paralysis as a realm of sleep in which your mind has regained consciousness before your rapid eye movement (REM) sleep has finished. I could sense and see things around me, but I could not move. I can remember this huge presence floating into the room and resting in my arms as if it knew me. There was no fear and the room was full of glory and peace. I was not afraid.

When I woke it was like Michela had been there in the room with me. I could smell her and feel her in my soul. It was then that the Holy Spirit boldly spoke into my soul. Of course, at the time, I shared this experience with no one. Even Courtney might have thought I was unstable and certifiably ready for inpatient treatment. But real or not real, true or not true, this is what I know. My brain was overwhelmed and exhausted. My thoughts and ways were rising up against the Word of God. My conscious and subconscious selves were battling. Compartmentalizing things had become very difficult for me. And the dream felt real. Period.

If your grieving loved one ever finds enough courage to entrust one of these encounters, these dreams, with you, your first response should always be silently praying. By this point of your journey, praying in silence will have become second nature to you. You will hopefully be so confident in your reliance on the Holy Spirit that you will be able to pray to Him even in the middle of an interaction with your grieving loved one, no matter the atmosphere. If you have not yet mastered this, continue working that muscle; it's a game-changer.

As you pray, listening to the encounter, the "dream," try your best to remain neutral. Your grieving loved one will probably say things to prepare you for the unusualness of what they are about to share, such as "I know this might sound crazy," or "I just wanted to ask your opinion, I know it's not true." Or they may come straight out and ask you, "Do you believe in angels or ghosts?" My only suggestion, other than silently praying, is to ask them to start with how their day began rather than jumping right into the dream. This way, if there was a trigger, you won't miss it. As in my example, understanding what the initial trigger was (finding a clean pair of Michela's undergarments in the dryer) will help you to assist in the validating of their claims and mental wellbeing.

Listen without making judgments. It does not matter if you believe or don't believe. Assess if the dream or encounter places your grieving loved one in immediate threat of harm. If there is no thought of hurting themselves or others, allow your grieving loved one to express what they believe they have experienced. If possible, say absolutely nothing. Use those nonverbal tools we have spoken about: a touch, a compassionate tilt of your head, or deep diaphragm breaths. Then conclude with a gentle "can we pray?" Keep the prayer short and positive. Focus on asking the Father to reveal His will in the dream. Ask Him to help your grieving loved one lean to His understanding and not their own. Thank Him for giving both you and your grieving loved one soundness of mind. Thank Him for continued peace, in Jesus' Holy Name. The enemy does not like spiritual progress. He will come up against you and your words. But he cannot come up against God. A God who does come to us in dreams. A God who did come to me in a way I had never experienced.

It was about ten years ago that He spoke to me so firmly, yet lovingly: "Jacqueline, as soon as you stop thinking about Michela as your earthly daughter, you will see her as she is today." I immediately thought of the scripture with Mary crying at the opened, borrowed tomb of Jesus.

I could visualize myself seated at the foot of Michela's passing over bed, crying and in complete shock over what she was or had been. Now, almost eighteen years after Michela passed on, it is these truths I have come to understand and trust. I was looking for Michela as I wanted her, which blurred my vision. Just like Mary, my grieving heart blocked my physical eyes from Michela's new presence, a presence that was easily hidden behind so much pain, anguish, and shock. My truths were patiently waiting for me, just as Jesus waited patiently at the entrance of His own borrowed tomb and allowed Mary's sorrowful and anguished heart time to comprehend who stood before her in John 20:11–18. Jesus had risen but not yet ascended. Mary's "master and teacher" was standing right before her (John 20:14). Trust the infallible Word of God, if not my tried and tested testimony. Jesus is standing right here, there, everywhere, patiently waiting for all those who are heavy-laden and burdened by the weight of grief. He, the Holy Spirit, is strategically positioned to detect and inject exactly what needs to be added or removed to allow the full truth of the Father's will to be received. Just as Mary eventually saw Jesus, and I eventually saw Michela, standing in due season, so will the path of your grieving loved one become clearer, too.

God has been so faithful in every promise He has given me. Although I would love to tell you it was an instantaneous transformation from that dream forward, I cannot. However, it was the beginning of my acceptance stage or phase. My words began to align more and more to those of the Holy Spirit. The Father's love was providing me tangible evidence; things were beginning to work according to His will and my expected end. I could almost believe that He could be able to heal my broken heart. My sorrow and depression lessened enough to allow hope in God, not in me, to take root. It was almost a partial or light-hearted acceptance that God might not be done with me yet. These words ring through the latter pages of my journal. Today, they provide me with even more clarity, as my journey is still evolving every day, leaving sorrow behind and moving toward the possibility of a better day than yesterday.

CHAPTER 6
Acceptance

The exhausting journey to acceptance leads us to depend upon His Word. Acceptance involves acknowledging the reality that our loved one is physically absent and recognizing that this new reality is permanent. As your grieving loved one begins to accept or accepts their physical reality through the guidance of the Holy Spirit, there will be spiritual evidence or fruit of their surrendering to God's infallible Word. We have already discussed the first and most apparent sign: the outward acknowledgment of God through spoken or verbally communicated acceptance. Their words or conversations will begin to change as the Holy Spirit begins to lead and teach them how to walk through the shadows of death. The Word teaches us that it is through spiritual warfare that we battle the trials and tribulations of this world. All those who love and believe in Jesus, all those who desire to understand the fullness of His Word for our lives, must eventually come to the same exact realization or acceptance that all God's children live and breathe by God's terms. Just as we think of ourselves as good earthly parents when we have great expectations for our children, the Word teaches how much sweeter is the love that flows from Him who created all things. It is this truth which brings us all running like children to our Heavenly Father. As we run toward acceptance, it brings us to a clearer understanding and confidence that regardless of how we feel, God's way is better. This is a truth we can trust, an everlasting, eternal truth that reigns over any and all permissible, temporary feelings of shock, denial, anger, guilt, and/or sorrow. Now, when and if we revisit these temporary emotions, we see and allow them according to our new references. We are not as we were at the beginning of this journey; we have learned what is and is not beneficial. And we choose, most often, to align ourselves to the Lord.

During this phase, less attention, energy, and time is spent on the need to understand (shock), question (denial), condemn (anger), accuse (guilt), or subdue (sorrow and/or depression), and more time is intentionally spent on embracing the Word of God. Conversations with your loved one will give witness to this. You will begin to hear the words flowing from a heart that chooses the truth, God's truth, over the weight of grief.

The second sign of acceptance will be your grieving loved one realizing the value of God in their life. The book of Job gives a great example as Job openly confesses this with his spoken words. Job came to the reality or acceptance of the truth and quickly chose to place all of his trust in God during his overwhelming situation. Job proclaims, "Even though he kills me, I'll continue to hope in him" (Job 13:15a, ISV). This is absolutely a marvelous sign of wellness. Therefore, when you begin to see your grieving loved one valuing the presence of God in their situation, you'll know that acceptance is here. The surrendering acceptance, deciding to not understand, but rather to lean on God's understanding, captures all shock, denial, anger, guilt, and sorrow, bringing them under submission to the Word. Yes, your grieving loved one might have times of revisiting some phases and stages. Nevertheless, you can trust the truth: God's infallible Word always accomplishes God's will and never returns void (Isaiah 55:11).

My permanent reality was aligned with a newfound understanding of my relationship with Michela moving forward. This reality was one that the Holy Spirit had so painfully revealed to me years ago, when my heart had not yet grown the spiritual muscles to receive it. These are muscles I have only grown because I endured the anguish of my journey. This was a most difficult thing for me to surrender, because in my mind, the Holy Spirit was requesting me to give Him something that rightfully belonged to me: my hopes, dreams, and memories of being the one thing I did and do great, mothering. This fact was so hidden in the recesses of my heart that only the skillful, delicate, intimate, and timeless patience of the Holy Spirit's touches could even begin to reveal it to me. He spent years and years gently persuading me to simply give

God a try. He steadfastly sought after me with confidence. Now, my heart was ready to receive God's healing message to me through the Holy Spirit: that Michela was now my sister in Christ Jesus. My ability to accept this truth would allow me to see Michela as she truly is.

Even today, this is the hardest request God has ever made of me, that I choose and accept my reborn relationship as Michela's sister in Christ Jesus. I understood completely what God was requesting of my heart. I began to pray for understanding and acceptance of the Father's will. Just as Job and David had to, we all must come to our own reality of God's truth in our present circumstance. Yes, the circumstances are hard and difficult to endure, just as were Job's circumstances as he lay in a bed, covered with sores, receiving the worst news any parent can receive, that all his children had been tragically killed. Those of us whose loved ones have passed over can understand the weight of grief Job must have been experiencing, to abruptly find himself without his seven sons and three daughters. We can even understand Job's questions after being blindly placed on this journey. Job questioned, saying, "How many are my iniquities and sins? Make me know my transgression and my sin. Why do You hide Your face, and regard me as Your enemy?" (Job 13:23–24, NKJV). I can remember being there, questioning God while seated in Arlington Memorial Hospital ER, asking, "Why are You allowing this?" But if you can believe that the Father has the power to allow this pain, you must also come to an acceptance, as Job did, as I did, that all suffering is not unto death, which forces us kicking and screaming toward "better." This is a very hard statement for me to say today, but hard does not mean false. This is what paralyzed me, more than anything, for so long. How could I ever come to say that Michela's passing over was good for me? Well, I still cannot say those words, but what I can say is "I trust God." I trust God that, in my childlike understanding, it is enough just to trust Him. Isn't that what a goodly child does, trust the truth of their earthly parents? Then, one day, your grieving loved one will do as David did and sing a new song. Eventually, as you become better and better at the implementation and application of our **Four Principles,** you will begin to hear and witness more and more signs of acceptance. Just as David and I did, your grieving loved one will begin to proclaim, for those of us who mourn, "Oh, sing to the Lord a new song! Sing to the Lord, all the earth" (Psalm 96:1, NKJV).

At this point in my journey, I am uncertain if I will always have times of grief over Michela as my daughter. Nevertheless, I am fully persuaded that I will rejoice forever in heaven with her as my sister in Christ Jesus. This is the level of acceptance your grieving loved one will experience during this season of their journey to and through grief. The back and forth with other stages might resurface, and it is okay to trust what has already been working. Continue to use the **Principles**, continue to pray, and lean not to your own understanding of your loved one's journey to and through grief. Be vigilant for those signs of acceptance, of trusting God's Word and proclaiming victory from their own lips. As we know, "out of the abundance of the heart the mouth speaketh" (Matthew 12:34b, KJV).

Many different things have caused different stages or phases to resurface over the years. These reasons are real and valid, such as when Michela's school-aged friends began to graduate college, get married, and start families of their own. Every time, as they walk away, there is a sorrow that visits me deep in my stomach. Sometimes, even after all these years, a smell or memory of that day revisits me and immediately I'm back to June 7, 2003. Some days I must continually ask the Father to help me surrender my thoughts and emotions to Him. There are still fleeting moments when thoughts just come and for a second I feel paralyzed. It is during these times that I have learned to trust God and endure, knowing that His grace is sufficient. When the hurt of what I was and can no longer be creeps up in my heart or mind, I quickly bring it under submission through the spoken confession from my mouth. I usually say something like, "God's Word is truth, all else is lies," or "I trust the truth of God's Word." I have learned through enduring my journey that these words work, helping me to bring my emotions and thoughts under control—or as my Bishop, Pastor T.D. Jakes, so powerfully proclaims, we "arrest" or "serve notice to" the enemy.

Mastery during this part of the journey will include seeing both signs of acceptance operating in agreement as your grieving loved one begins to fully apply the power of trusting and valuing God's thoughts and ways over their own. When you hear the testimony of faith from their mouth, the first sign of acceptance, this is movement in the right direction. The second sign is action-based—your grieving loved one will begin to acknowledge God with their actions. Their eyes and ears will begin to seek being with God more and more. Less and less time will be spent on or in the past. Your grieving loved one will begin to purposefully reopen their heart to the possibility of loving fully again. They will start to walk each day in acceptance. Through the guidance of the Holy Spirit, your grieving loved one will find ways to enjoy life again, in spite of the pain they have had and are experiencing. This does not mean they will never again visit the other stages and phases of grief; rather, as with all of God's children, they will be moving toward being better and better each day. This type of grief does not just magically or totally disappear; but in this stage, there is a purposeful choice to stand on the truth that can be trusted. Healing happens as we find healthy ways of expressing and releasing our emotions. Like the other stages, there are blends or levels of acceptance.

Acceptance can visit your grieving loved one's heart at any time for any reason. The depth of magnitude can and will vary, too. There may be a little acceptance today, but no evidence of acceptance tomorrow. They may be completely accepting over morning coffee, and then searching for acceptance by noon. You have to be ready to revisit stages and prepared for grief to resurface. These are not setbacks, but rather setups, each one bringing your grieving loved one closer and closer to full acceptance. My experiences of healing have lasted over the course of eighteen years, and I am still growing better and better each day. I now understand that acceptance was always here awaiting me, even when my weeping, grief-stricken eyes could not see. The question now is, can I really rejoice, and again rejoice?

Transitory Blending Phase

As your grieving loved one begins to transition from acceptance to the final stage of their grief journey, you will begin to regularly and routinely hear and see your grieving loved one's outward expressions of faith more fully and completely. You will begin to be needed less and less as your grieving loved one begins to rely more and more on the Holy Spirit. It is at this point that you will need to readjust your thinking, prayer life, and attitudes toward a healthy separation. After spending so many months, and sometimes years, being so intimately committed to the care of someone, it can leave you feeling unwanted or even emotionally depleted. When first called to service, you committed to standing in a position of intercession for your loved one. But gradually, as with those I have come to support along their journeys, you will begin to feel less and less needed. The late-night emergency calls have all but stopped. The outbursts and questions have now been surrendered to the purposeful acceptance of the Father's will. The emotional ups and downs have leveled off, and days, sometimes months, pass without the once-daily needed reminders that God is in control. You are now able to provide more meat to your conversations. Those scriptures which have become your cornerstones throughout this process have become embodied. You will now be able to give testimony, just as I. Your sight will no longer be murky and you will clearly be able to see, like Simon of Cyrene, just how strategically God had positioned you.

During this part of the journey, you will begin to understand the outwardly expression of acknowledging God and valuing His thoughts and ways over all other feelings. No emotion, doctrine, or viewpoint dares to come against the lessons you have been taught during this process. Your grieving loved one is now ready to engage each day with the passion and energy that comes from surviving with grace.

CHAPTER 7

Engaging in Life

At this point in your journey, let me proclaim victory! Well done, my good and faithful servant! You have endured through the stages of grief with your loved one, and now you can see the Father's perfect and expected end with more clarity. I believe that engaging in life is a purposeful promise available to all God's children after suffering. It is my hope, as with those who have supported me throughout my journey, that you have been changed as well. It is amazing how the Father has worked so many things out for my good over the last eighteen years. I'm always floored, in a state of awe, when blessed to hear the testimonies of my supporters. As they give their own personal accounts of things they have learned and experienced through my suffering, it becomes apparent that most have come to a new level of trusting the truth. It is during this stage of your grieving loved one's journey that they are ready. They are better able to stand firmly on those strong, spiritual muscles that God has been developing throughout this entire process. Just as the Holy Spirit guided you to this book, be "confident of this very thing, that He who began a good work in you will perfect it until the day of Christ Jesus" (Philippians 1:6, NASB). Just as Simon of Cyrene's time to assist Jesus in His weighted cross journey eventually came to an end, so will your time come to surrender your position as a supporter. As your grieving loved one begins to exhibit clear signs of acceptance, their newfound reliance on God's perfect truth and will for their lives will draw them closer to Him.

I have had many people who have supported me to and through my journey, but not everyone has endured the entire course. Those who have, whose deeds were led by the Holy Spirit, will be rewarded in heaven. For others, whose hearts were not pure or whose motives did not align with God's perfect plan, their actions and deeds, whether innocent or malicious, have all been swept away. Therefore, we concern ourselves not with those who came and went, for the Word states, "They went out from us, but they did not really belong to us. For if they had belonged to us, they would have remained with us; but their going showed that none of them belonged to us" (1 John 2:19, NIV). When standing in peace with all those who have come or not come, left or stayed, it is important for us to remember Simon of Cyrene. He was ordained and empowered by the Holy Spirit to come out of the crowd. Therefore, we cast our cares of who did not come when called, or who came that were not called, on the Father. And we give thanks to Him, from whom all blessings flow, for those like you and Simon of Cyrene. Although in my grief journey Ron's and Hilary's deeds were noteworthy, we are equally grateful for all those, small and great, who have supported and assisted in any way. Journeys like these are bumpy and rocky, full of potholes and detours. It's a journey which until recently seemed impossible in the mind and heart of your grieving loved one. Now, at the end of the journey, there's tangible evidence and signs that the consuming and overwhelming seasons of shock, denial, anger, guilt, and sorrow have been taken captive and are now operating under the obedience of Christ (2 Corinthians 10:5).

We can begin to position ourselves toward being a victorious conqueror. One way to accomplish this is to be forgiving. The enemy, and sometimes our own flesh, can be overly critical of those who did leave, or hurt and bruised by those who stayed for selfish motives and reasons. A child of God must be able to forgive. This might become difficult as your grieving loved one has time to process things more clearly. As their grief-centered perspective comes more and more under submission, they will also begin to see and remember those distractions and traps the enemy used along their journey.

I can remember one of my close friends getting upset with me during the first few years of my journey. One day she became so angry at me, she shouted, "You didn't even tell me thank you for all I did when Michela passed away." During the early years of my journey, this separated us and caused a huge problem within our relationship. I stopped speaking with this person and felt I had every right to do so. Others agreed with me. How could anyone, especially a friend, expect me to have the mindset or energy to be thankful during the worst time of my life? How could she expect me to be so present? Wasn't the whole purpose of having her around to care for me? Did her words mean that she had hate or envy in her heart toward me? Nope; I choose to believe the best of her. Just as with Job's friends, she had no reference to assist me through my pain. She was just attempting to understand and assisted using all she had at the time. Learning to think the best of people's efforts helps to keep you moving forward. The dangers involved in hanging on to or even digging up old hurts and pains are too great, especially because under close evaluation, we all have come to understand that none of us had any personal references to guide us.

My heart was so sick, it has taken over eighteen years for the personalized, intimate, restorative care from the Holy Spirit to get me here. There is no person who could have completed this task but God. I tell you this because the enemy will attempt to use past hurts and pains to derail God's good work. A position of forgiveness is a choice we can make to, "If it be possible, as much as lieth in you, live peaceably with all men" (Romans 12:18, KJV). My friend was like the three men who ran to Job's bedside; they were leaning to their own understanding. When things go wrong in our lives, our natural response is to seek answers. They were attempting to rationalize the sovereignty of God using their own thoughts and ways. But those answers were truths that God has strategically positioned, even hidden, to be revealed in the most peculiar places along the journey. They were answers that were locked deep in Job's heart. They are answers like my need to still be Michela's mother. These answers are hidden so deep within the heart, only God can search them out.

Each and every believer must come to the fullness of God's expected plan for their lives. I have completely and fully forgiven all those who knowingly and unknowingly caused me harm, hurt, pain, and, yes, even doubt. I can forgive them because regardless of the outcomes or motives, whether good or bad, everyone has done their best. But the ultimate reason for my universal forgiveness viewpoint is "to God be the Glory." I give all credit to God and His completed work on the cross, as well as His eternal forethought on my behalf to position the Holy Spirit right in the middle of the action.

You should be actively looking for signs of forgiveness in the life of your grieving loved one. Forgiveness is the best universal sign that your grieving loved one has accepted God's will and is engaging in the fullness of God's expected future. When acceptance begins to truly and freely flow, there will be a supernatural overflow of acceptance. This overflow will sprout out of your grieving loved one's soul as engagement. You will see evidence of them engaging in the fullness of life as God has purposed and planned. Your grieving loved one will begin to reach upward to God.

Most grief journeys begin with sleepless nights and endless questioning (i.e. why is this happening to my child? Does scripture not apply to my situation? Where is God?) and the overwhelming need to be close to the memories of the past (going to the gravesite, playing soulful music, spending hours crying over old photos and videos). Now you will begin to see and experience your grieving loved one intentionally reaching out to God. You will see them grabbing and balancing themselves on the power of God's living Word. The seeds from each and every stage or phase have sprung forth with deep, rich roots. The Word has taken possession of their once sick, hope-deferred heart, and now gives tried and tested, firsthand accounts of the goodness of God. "I had fainted, unless I had believed to see the goodness of the Lord in the land of the living" (Psalm 27:13, KJV). Your grieving loved one will begin to measure their day not according to the trials and tribulations of this world, but rather according to the infallible Word of God. As this begins to occur, you may witness what you believe to be "setbacks." Trust me, in the body of Christ, for His children, these are not setbacks, but rather an opportunity for the Holy Spirit to correct thinking, attitudes, and hearts toward His ultimate plan: the glorification of God.

You may still be witnessing what some have termed, in regards to my worship, as "too much," "overdoing," or "eccentric" praise. My spiritual, professional, and personal advice would be to continue to utilize being silent and praying. I can remember a time when every word which flowed from my mouth was scripture in some way, shape, or form. I felt like anything else would lead me to a relapse. But balance will come and this, too, shall pass. God's living Word draws and leads us to being ever present with Him, where our help and strength for the daily cares of this world can be found. Eventually, in God's perfect timing, He will give your grieving loved one the same choice He gave his disciples. Who do you say I am? As your grieving loved one's heart ponders over this, as His disciples did, they will come to their own answers based on their own personal journey and experience to and through this process.

I felt so fragile during my early moments of engaging in life. I would repeat over and over, "All else is a lie." I must have said this small yet effectual truth over a million times since Michela's passing over. But it has provided the framework for what I am today: totally and completely persuaded that God is sovereign. All shock, denial, anger, guilt, and sorrow must be quickly cast on Him. As I stand before you today, writing, it can still be very difficult, not having Michela here, not seeing her amazing smile or hearing her lovely voice. But as your grieving loved one has learned or will learn, nothing can separate us from the love of God, not even death, as is proclaimed to us in Romans 8:35–39. I believe that the biggest step for me was walking away from what I had planned and finding the strength to actually believe I could ever be happy, content, and prosperous in life without Michela. I testify to you today that I am. I stand in agreement that using the **Principles** we have discussed throughout this book will assist not only your grieving loved one, but you as well.

We were never given the ability to heal our own hearts, and are thereby invited to and expected by God to surrender all to Him. Those of us who are parents understand this completely. Although we love our children and want them to experience only the best of life, as good parents, we understand that we must prepare them for all of life, including trials and tribulations. It is during these seasons or parts of our journey that we learn God's voice and character. This is also when we begin to master how to quickly surrender and lean on those things which can be eternally trusted. It is during these times that many of God's children find their God-given purpose. Engaging in life does not mean there will never again be hurt, pain, or even new questions. It does mean we are equipped to count it all joy (James 1:2). It does mean that your grieving loved one's engagement with their new reality and circumstances will be looked upon based on God's infallible Word. Instead of trusting and relying on their emotions or even their own earthly sensations, your grieving loved one will choose to trust the truth. The words in Jeremiah 29:11 will become their living testimony. They have learned and will continue to learn how to always seek

God's expected plan and desires. They will implement this truth in all situations, regardless of how they feel, knowing that He will never harm them. It does not matter, as Job gives testimony, how we feel. We must be "confident of this very thing, that He which hath begun a good work in you will perform it until the day of Jesus Christ" (Philippians 1:6, KJV). I have to admit, when I began writing this book, many people thought I should provide more of a scientific, research-based viewpoint. But I stand before you, engaged in life, not because of science (which I love) or research (which I also love). I stand before you today simply because God is bigger, and He knew His plans for me. He refused to leave me and He has never forsaken me.

I stand before you today because God did all He told me He would accomplish and more. I stand before you, engaged in my life, writing, teaching, volunteering, loving, protecting, and encouraging. Just like Shadrach, Meshach, and Abednego, I have emerged from my fiery furnace because of the presence of God in my life. I have no permanent signs of my dramatic past, or of my experiences with shock, denial, anger, guilt, or sorrow. I stand before you because God not only refused to leave me, He sent Pastor Myers to come get me out of my stinky bed. He used Michela's Bible to remind me that He is Lord over all things, including death and the grave. He opened my weary eyes and told me, "Jacqueline, Michela is not as you once knew her." He patiently allowed me to be angry and upset. He allowed me to say things and call Him things He knew I didn't mean, all because I needed to come full circle with how and who Michela loved the most: her Heavenly Father.

It has been many years for me. I can't tell you how long it will take for your grieving loved one's sick, hope-deferred heart to begin to engage with life once again. I will tell you that these principles work. I will tell you that beauty for ashes and a garment of praise are available to all those who mourn. I can testify that God has always done the work. I can testify that being silent is okay. I can also give testimony that this book was meant for you. As stated in the introduction, if you allow, your help is here. I apologize to no one and nothing for my complete and unwavering confidence in God's ability to take care of all His children. I can testify that my journey through grief has been solely mine; it was tailor-made for me. Only the Holy Spirit is qualified to provide complete comfort. The strategically positioned placement of the Holy Spirit is intentional, placing Him directly on the scene to be a present help in our times of need. "But the Comforter, which is the Holy Ghost, whom the Father will send in My name, He shall teach you all things, and bring all things to your remembrance, whatsoever I have said unto you" (John 14:26, KJV).

One really good example of this truth occurred on a recent Saturday at Cedar Hill Preservation with my hiking buddy. This person is one of my daily prayer partners and supporters, and also has the same birth date as Michela's passing. We have a hiking location which we have come to call "The Stairway to Heaven." It is a very steep and rocky climb, even for those of us who visit it often. We made it almost 90 percent of the way up when my partner, who usually leads us on our weekly hikes, stopped. Her pause was more than fine with me as the air seemed to be abnormally thick. At the same time, we both gazed back and smiled at each other, because we had come so far. It was then that the Holy Spirit brought my journey back to my remembrance. That day, just as Jesus proclaimed, the Holy Spirit spoke life into both of our souls so softly. It was like the Holy Spirit was quietly speaking to both of our hearts in unison: "Yes, you have come so far." Even though we still had more climbing ahead of us to reach the magnificent view which awaited us at the top, the climb seemed so much easier. We reached the top, as we do with every climb. But this time we had received individualized encouragement from the Father. Trust the truth; God is here, God cares, and God has a plan for all things involving His children. Look back often in acknowledgment of God in all your ways, and He will direct your path (Proverbs 3:6).

As you begin to view and witness your grieving loved one's reliance and acceptance as they begin to trust the truth more and more, I encourage you to continue applying your **Principles**, especially if any opposing feelings arise, which they may. It is okay. Sometimes, when we have been pouring so much time, energy, and love into someone else, our own paths become a little neglected or weedy. This can bring up feelings of resentment if we are not careful. It is also true that the enemy is looking for those he can devour, and because you love God and have been selected to do His will, you can believe that you are considered by the devil to be public enemy number one. But although this is true, the work you have done has been recorded in heavenly places. Regardless of the attacks or considerations of the enemy, your prayers and the accomplishments you have made have come and are coming into full fruition. We will not allow any person, place, or thing to tell or testify otherwise. All relationships which align with the Word of God are healthy, full, and complete, lacking nothing. Trust the completed work of the Holy Spirit. In this type of spirit-filled communication, you will begin to witness it pouring from the heart and mouth of your grieving loved one as they begin to speak and meditate on more and more things of good report (Philippians 4:8, KJV) instead of things of the past.

As the supporter of someone who is grieving, we forget that spiritual warfare is exhausting and sometimes seemingly impossible when using our own strengths and capabilities. Sometimes, as the supporter, we forget to care, love, and pray for ourselves. As we close our wonderful journey together, I would like to once again thank you for standing in commitment with those who are mourning. Your intercession is, has been, or will be, according to scripture, one of the best gifts of faith we can share one to another. You are, have been, or will be the comforting touch of the Father in someone's present time of need. Remember to pray for yourself without ceasing, knowing that the effectual prayers of the righteous avail much, even the overshadowing stages and phases of shock, denial, anger, guilt, and sorrow. We are completely confident that the victory belongs to God. Return to the **Quick Reference Guide** as much as needed. You might need it daily during the initial stages and phases of the journey, and you might not need it for years during other parts. Either way, seeking wisdom is another sign of a healthy and fully engaged life. Please receive this closing prayer; it is for you. When you have days of doubt or disappointment, come back to this prayer; it will help to ease your burdens as I stand with you in agreement and as we prayerfully await the return of Jesus Christ.

Prayer for the Supporter

Heavenly Father,

I come before you today because you are the great "I AM," the kind of good parent that all children who believe in your Son's life, death, and resurrection can freely come to.

We honor Your ways and Your thoughts.

We confess that we can do nothing without Your guidance through the Holy Spirit.

We confess that we have sinned and fallen short of Your glory.

We accept Your cleansing, sanctifying power to make us more like You.

We come before You in prayer, asking for help to continuously cast all cares unto You.

Give us eyes to see.

Give us ears to hear.

Give us confidence to trust in the truth we have learned and will come to learn in and through spending time in Your Word.

Help us to lean to those truths and to freely give work to you today.

Help me to wait for You before I speak.

Help me to trust You while I remain quiet.

Help me to allow _____ (the name of your grieving loved one) to hear your thoughts and ways over others.

Help me to apply the principles which I have learned.

Help me to rest when tired, knowing You never faint or slumber.

Thank You for being an ever-present help in our times of trouble.

Thank You for protecting my family, provisions, and purposes while my heart is working in the preparation of the Gospel.

I trust the truth, and all else is a lie. I am a child of the Living King, and nothing shall separate me from that love.

In the Name of Jesus, the author and finisher of our faith, Amen.

Quick Reference Guide

CONFESSION OF FAITH

If you are not saved, or are not sure you are saved, it is important to understand where you stand concerning the promises of God. Yes, God loves all people. And yes, God's Word applies to any and all situations. But there are conditions to salvation for those of us considered Gentiles, or non-Jews. The Jewish people are God's chosen people. The term *Gentiles* encompasses all others. As Gentiles, John 3:16 is one of the most important scriptures in the Bible. It gives us access and guarantees our legitimacy as heirs of God. Therefore, this is one of the most important sections within the entire book. Are you saved? Do you have the assurances and privileges that accompany accepting Jesus into your heart as Lord and Savior?

If you do, please pray for those who are not saved who are reading or will read these words. Pray that they come to the Father and accept Him right now.

If you are uncertain, please take this opportunity to receive Him into your heart as Lord and Savior.

If you don't, please consider what this means. You are uncovered. You are like a leaf blowing in the wind. You are outside of the protection afforded to God's children. And yes, you will die and be separated from God for eternity. You will also be separated from those saved loved ones who have accepted Jesus as Lord.

The Good News for us all is that through His blood, Jesus has made a universal way for us all to come to the Father. It is available to you right now. If you are not saved, or are saved and feel compelled to recommit, please read the following scriptures:

- If you confess that Jesus is Lord and believe that God raised him from death, you will be saved. For it is by our faith that we are put right with God; it is by our confession that we are saved. (Romans 10:9–10, GNT)
- For God so loved the world that he gave his one and only Son, that whoever believes in him shall not perish but have eternal life. (John 3:16, NIV)
- For whosoever shall call upon the name of the Lord shall be saved. (Romans 10:13, KJV)
- But as many as received him, to them gave he power to become the sons of God, even to them that believe on his name. (John 1:12, KJV)
- Therefore if any man be in Christ, he is a new creature: old things are passed away; behold, all things are become new. (2 Corinthians 5:17, KJV)

Do you believe?

If so, please read the confession of faith out loud into the atmosphere.

If not yet or not now, please continue to meditate on the above scriptures and pray. The master teacher, the Holy Spirit, is available and ready. Just continue seeking.

Confession of Faith Prayer

Dear God, I am a sinner and need your forgiveness. I believe that Jesus Christ shed His precious blood and died for my sin. I am willing to change and turn from my sin. I now invite Jesus Christ to come into my heart and life as my personal Savior.

Amen

Principles

Principle 1: The work belongs to God.

Principle 2: Silence is more than okay, it is vital.

Principle 3: The Holy Spirit is the master teacher.

Principle 4: The journey belongs to your grieving loved one.

These **Principles** are truths that can, should, and will be used by you throughout all stages or phases of grief. Write them down, speak them out of your mouth, pray over them, and apply them. Principles are effectual, but without implementation, they cannot help.

SHOCK

Shock is the body's protective mechanism that kicks in to prevent the griever from being completely overwhelmed by the devastating news they have received. There is no magical formula to move someone on from shock. Shock is typical. The griever may talk about, or you may observe them experiencing, feelings of being "on autopilot." Some grievers experience an inability to cry. Others may not be able to stop crying. All emotions or lack of emotions are welcomed during these early moments of experiencing the pain of loss. Like all stages of grief, the foggy, numbing realization is the body's protective mechanism and is completely normal. The surest sign that you are dealing with shock is questioning from the griever.

JOURNEY PATTERNS

1. Questioning: The griever will ask things like, "Why is this happening to me?" "Where is God?" "Why did my loved one have to die?" and, in cases of suicide, "Does suicide mean this individual is condemned to hell?"
2. Numbness or uncontrollable weeping: You may hear things such as, "I am okay; it is just life," "They are in a better place," "I will see them again," "I

cannot believe they are gone," "I cannot cry anymore," or "The tears will not come out."

APPLICATION

Apply **Principle 1:** The work belongs to God, and **Principle 2:** Silence is more than okay, it is vital.

There is nothing that words or actions can do to convince or reason away a broken heart. Apply **Principle 1** and **Principle 2** often during this season. Do not be afraid of silence. Remember, it is more than okay, it is vital. Spoken words will not penetrate a traumatically broken heart. Use nonverbal gestures to communicate your support. Remember the acronym E.M.P.A.T.H.Y.:

> **E:** eye contact; making eye contact is important. Practice just looking and being present in a mirror.

> **M:** muscles of your facial expression; you will hear things that might seem different or unusual. The key is learning to softly nod your head in agreement and not show disagreement.

> **P:** posture; at times this is more important than speaking. Adopt an open and welcoming posture: arms open, leaning in, shoulders down, and seated or kneeling.

> **A:** affect; wait to see how one nonverbal cue affects the griever before initiating another. You might reach out for their hand, but have them draw it back. Don't force

it. Take deep diaphragm breaths (another nonverbal cue) and see if it is received differently. This is not a science. Be patient with yourself and your grieving loved one.

T: tone of voice; your tone should be so soft, it is almost silent. Remember **Principle 2**.

H: hearing; hearing from the Holy Spirit is the most important thing here. I have learned how to commune with the Holy Spirit in the middle of all conversations. You will need to practice this and utilize it often during this journey. It's one of those gifts that will keep on giving. Pray to the Father and ask Him to give you ears to hear Him over any and all persons and things, then practice it, master it, and experience a new kind of awareness.

Y: your response should always be to pray first. Just get into the habit. Ask, "Can we pray?" Nothing, absolutely nothing, is better than prayer.

Truth to Trust

- The effectual fervent prayer of a righteous man availeth much. (James 5:16b, KJV)
- And the peace of God, which surpasses all understanding, will guard your hearts and your minds in Christ Jesus. (Philippians 4:7, ESV)

- Blessed are those who mourn, for they shall be comforted. (Matthew 5:4, ESV)
- And now these three remain: faith, hope, and love. But the greatest of these is love. (1 Corinthians 13:13, NIV)
- A new commandment I give unto you, that ye love one another; as I have loved you, that ye also love one another. (John 13:34, KJV)
- And he said unto me, "My grace is sufficient for thee: for my strength is made perfect in weakness." Most gladly therefore will I rather glory in my infirmities, that the power of Christ may rest upon me. (2 Corinthians 12:9, KJV)
- For God has not given us a spirit of fear, but of power and of love and of a sound mind. (2 Timothy 1:7, NKJV)

Prayer for Shock

Father, we come to You because You are the great I Am. You are the beginning, middle, and end of all things great and small. You are the Alpha and Omega. You are all knowing and all powerful. Your words tell us that the fervent prayers of the righteous availeth much. Thank You for making us righteous that we might come before You in intercessory prayer for _____ (grieving loved one).

Your Word teaches us that a peace that surpasses all understanding is available for those who seek and trust in You. You tell us that those who mourn are blessed and will be comforted. You tell us that Your grace is sufficient in our times of trouble and that Your strength is made perfect in our weaknesses. As we bring _____ (grieving loved one's) heart and mind to You, we request peace, power, and a sound mind. We request for our eyes to be opened in Your perfect timing to see Your perfect answer to all questions.

Strengthen us to apply Your truths. Strengthen us to trust those truths. It is in Your Son's Name, Jesus our Lord and Savior, in which we pray.

Amen

DENIAL

Different people will have different approaches when dealing with denial—which is okay. There are no wrongs or rights here! We are all finding our way, pressing to and through the journey in its time and in due season. Time produces familiarity with this journey. The daily application and practice of these principles will begin to provide new, tried and tested references unique to you. After eighteen years on this journey, I trust God's sovereign presence to overcome all grief-based denial. It is important for now for you to remain present, offering your grieving loved one opportunities to enjoy simple things without pressure, such as setting dates for lunch at the park. Denial can bring on a range of emotions and actions which might seem morally, ethically, or spiritually wrong. Just listen and allow your grieving loved one's words to be heard. Use your nonverbal communication skills, such as making eye contact, touching the hand or shoulder, and asking to pray with them. Your goal here is to patiently and observantly watch and intercede. Trust the Holy Spirit to speak to those conflicting voices as you position yourself to never cease from praying.

Journey Patterns

1. Aftershock: Your grieving loved one is moving from the protective mechanism of shock into the subtle or forceful grasp of denial. The level of denial can depend on many factors associated with the loss. The most important thing to remember is that the brain and heart are attempting to find points of reference after being completely disjointed.

2. Avoidance of the present: Your grieving loved one might avoid discussing or acknowledging their pain. Conversation might be superficial and shallow in nature. It is okay; just because words are not being spoken does not mean the Holy Spirit is not working. The most meaningful conversation right now is between your grieving loved one's heart and the Master Comforter. Trust the truth.

3. Isolation: Your grieving loved one might begin to pull away from family and friends. It might become difficult to connect with them. You might have to

work a little harder or be a little firmer here. Try to give your grieving loved one options, such as asking if they would like to go for lunch or meet early for breakfast. This gives your grieving loved one a sense of control in a time when they might feel victimized by their current journey. You will have to be long-suffering and forgiving during this season. Remember, it is not about you. This is not your cross to carry.

4. Overuse to cope: Your grieving loved one might over-exercise, overwork, and/or use alcohol to drown out or silence the voices of denial. Seek balance and moderation, rather than the elimination of any habit or temporary coping need that is not warranted. Allow your grieving loved one space to deal with their denial. Only the Holy Spirit can satisfy the longings and questions of a heart whose hope has been deferred. Your debate or reasoning only frustrates the situation. Silence is golden here. If help is needed, please do not hesitate to reach out to the proper professional. We have used family, behavioral, and spiritual counselors and therapists during every step of our journey. The reason does not matter. If you ever feel ill-equipped or led to get additional help, you should follow through with those feelings. Part of being a committed and diligent supporter is making those difficult decisions if and when they are needed.

APPLICATION

Apply **Principle 2:** Silence is more than okay, it is vital, and **Principle 4:** The Holy Spirit is the master teacher.

Just as with shock, the biggest and best voice here needs to be the Holy Spirit. Pray for strength to reduce your words as you master **Principle 2**. It is very easy to injure your grieving loved one during this season of their journey. Trust in the Holy Spirit, who has been strategically positioned by the Father right in the middle of the situation.

TRUTH TO TRUST

- For I know the thoughts that I think toward you, saith the Lord, thoughts of peace, and not of evil, to give you an expected end. (Jeremiah 29:11, KJV)
- And he who searches our hearts knows the mind of the Spirit, because the Spirit intercedes for God's people in accordance with the will of God. (Romans 8:27, NIV)
- The Spirit of God, who raised Jesus from the dead, lives in you. And just as God raised Christ Jesus from the dead, he will give life to your mortal bodies by this same Spirit living within you. (Romans 8:11, NLT)
- Being confident of this very thing, that he which hath begun a good work in you will perform it until the day of Jesus Christ. (Philippians 1:6, KJV)

- Be strong and courageous. Do not be afraid or terrified because of them, for the Lord your God goes with you; he will never leave you nor forsake you. (Deuteronomy 31:6, NIV)
- Thou shalt have no other gods before me. (Exodus 20:3, KJV)
- Casting down imaginations, and every high thing that exalteth itself against the knowledge of God, and bringing into captivity every thought to the obedience of Christ. (2 Corinthians 10:5, KJV)

Prayer for Denial

Father, we come to You because You are the great I Am. You are the beginning, the middle, and the end of all things great and small. You are the Alpha and the Omega. You are all-knowing and all-powerful. Your Word tells us that the fervent prayers of the righteous man availeth much, so we come to You for Your wisdom, love, and favor. Thank You for making us righteous that we might come before You in intercession for _____ (grieving loved one).

Your Word teaches us that You have an expected end for Your children, and nothing shall be impossible unto You. Your Word declares the work of the Holy Spirit, searches our hearts, and knows the mind of the Spirit. Thank You that the Holy Spirit is interceding for _____ (grieving loved one) in accordance to Your will. Strengthen my confidence in this very thing, that He which hath begun a good work in _____ (grieving loved one) will perform it until the day of Jesus Christ. Help me to be strong and courageous as I seek Your guidance to be still and to not be afraid. Help me to stand on Your promises and trust in them. I trust that, even when I am not there with _____ (grieving loved one), You are always available because Your Word says that You will never leave us or forsake us.

Your Word commands us to have no other gods before You. Therefore, we trust the truth that You will cast down all of _____ (grieving loved one's) imaginations and every high thing that exalteth itself against the knowledge of You, and bring into captivity every thought to obedience in Christ. This includes denial and its aftershock, which _____ (grieving loved one) may not be able to clearly see. We trust You. We wait on You. Strengthen me to apply Your truths in which I can trust. It is in Your Son's Name, Jesus our Lord and Savior, in which we pray.

Amen

Anger

Anger is one of the more transparent signs and symptoms you will experience while supporting your grieving loved one. As with all the other stages and phases, we intercede using our **Principles**. Just as with the other stages and phases we have discussed thus far, anger blurs your grieving loved one's already overstimulated brain. It causes your grieving loved one's emotional state to overflow. Come against negative or evil words and actions with prayer. Anger will hinder your loved one from mourning and, yes, even praying or seeking God. However, the Holy Spirit is strategically positioned right where the anger has found root. Only the Holy Spirit can see the root causes associated with your grieving loved one's anger. Allowing this anger to remain unchecked for too long can be detrimental, but the Mighty Comforter is located right on the scene. God has not forsaken your grieving loved one. God has not abandoned your grieving loved one. God has not turned a deaf ear to the cries and groans of your grieving loved one.

During periods of anger, a grieving person may be angry at themselves for their response to grief, or because they were unable to do anything to prevent the death. If the griever were to stop and think rationally, these feelings would not make sense, but they exist nonetheless. It is far better to work through them than to stuff them inside. The anger might be based on facts or on a mistruth like the one I held for so many months, that God was cruel and biased. Regardless of the origin, every high thing (or what seems high to our tired and overwhelmed hearts and minds) that exalts itself against the knowledge of God will be brought into captivity (2 Corinthians 10:5). Remain steadfast, forgive quickly, and plant seeds of gratitude. When your grieving loved one is angry at the person who passed over for leaving, find something to remind them how grateful you are that they continue to fight the good fight of faith (1 Timothy 6:12). Remember to implement more nonverbal forms of gratitude, such as a personalized card on a pillow, windshield, or door; an evening walk in silence; and/or an opportunity for your grieving loved one to rant without judgment. As the supporter, you should commit yourself to implementing the **Principles** you have mastered and to remember that love "keeps no record of wrongs" (1 Corinthians 13:5c, NIV).

Journey Patterns

1. Outbursts or lack of emotions: Your grieving loved one is moving from the protective season of denial to realizations which might align more with the truth, but which are still blurred. They might have a complete meltdown with all the trimmings, such as throwing things, beating their hands on their head, or breaking seemingly valued possessions. Or, they may not show any signs of aggression, being overly calm or almost detached from the present. All these are typical reactions for you to prayerfully watch, intervening only when professional assistance might be needed. Limit your words, and if you feel something might be off—for example, that you're seeing signs of complicated grief—immediately reach out for assistance. You may find that your grieving

loved one avoids discussing or acknowledging their pain, or shows an avoidance of the present. Conversation might be superficial and shallow in nature. It is okay; just because words are not being spoken does not mean that the Holy Spirit is not working. The most meaningful conversation right now is between your grieving loved one's heart and the Master Comforter. Trust the truth.

2. Resentment: Your grieving loved one may resent those who were involved, directly or indirectly, with the passing, or the resentment might be focused on something completely unrelated. I remember having hateful feelings if I saw a mother playing in the park with her children. I would get so hurt by the sounds of other families' happiness and resentful over the unanswered questions of why me? Why my family? Why Michela? Unanswered questions soiled in anger will eventually become resentment. Deal with anger in prayer and derail it with peaceful solutions, as this prevents anger from developing into full-blown resentment. This is one reason why The WARM Place was so helpful for our family. It gave us a place to say those things out loud in safety. Allow your grieving loved one a place to deal with feelings of resentment. Remember to continue working with the **Principles.** Modeling forgiveness and showing gratitude are also very good support tools for those on this journey.

3. Verbal abuse: The words from a broken-hearted person can be very cruel. It is important to remember at this time that darkness cannot overcome light. If your grieving loved one begins to name call or say hurtful things, do not engage, even with the Word. Give them space and time to commune with the Holy Spirit. It is very difficult to stay focused on implementing the **Principles** of this book while under verbal attack. It is okay to back away for a moment and pray. It is okay to allow the griever to spend some time with their own thoughts and emotions without feeling they are being examined. Remember to seek balance and moderation to help you determine if things are moving forward, are stagnant, or are disintegrating. It is okay to have feelings of anger. But, just as with guilt and denial, it is important to allow the grieving person space and time to seek God. If an incident of verbal abuse occurs, it is not okay. Just because someone is hurting does not give them a green light to hurt others. But it is important to have clarity and the ability to discern whether such outbursts are rare, or whether the griever has been having these types of incidents with everyone or for several months. These types of intimate, caring questions will help you to determine the peacemaker's course of action. It is important to have an intimate, non-judgmental approach to ensuring your grieving loved one is okay.

Being angry around anniversary dates, milestones of other family members, or even friends is not uncommon. Temporarily swinging like a pendulum to and from anger is no huge sign for alarm during the initial days and months. But being unable to move on from anger over the course of years is not healthy and should be addressed with love. Approach it with the same prayerful stance you have learned to apply throughout this book. Trust the truth.

Application

Apply all four **Principles** here: **Principle 1:** The work belongs to God, **Principle 2:** Silence is more than okay, it is vital, **Principle 3:** The Holy Spirit is the master teacher, and **Principle 4:** The journey belongs to your grieving loved one. Allow these **Principles** to pull you more and more toward your ultimate goal through prayer and supplication as you quietly observe to ensure your grieving loved one does not require professional intervention. If no professional attention is required, continue your position of interceding and not intervening.

Truth to Trust

- For I know the thoughts that I think toward you, saith the Lord, thoughts of peace, and not of evil, to give you an expected end. (Jeremiah 29:11, KJV)

- And he who searches our hearts knows the mind of the Spirit, because the Spirit intercedes for God's people in accordance with the will of God. (Romans 8:27, NIV)
- The Spirit of God, who raised Jesus from the dead, lives in you. And just as God raised Christ Jesus from the dead, he will give life to your mortal bodies by this same Spirit living within you. (Romans 8:11, NLT)
- Being confident of this very thing, that he which hath begun a good work in you will perform it until the day of Jesus Christ. (Philippians 1:6, KJV)
- Be strong and courageous. Do not be afraid or terrified because of them, for the Lord your God goes with you; he will never leave you nor forsake you. (Deuteronomy 31:6, NIV)
- Thou shalt have no other gods before me. (Exodus 20:3, KJV)
- Casting down imaginations, and every high thing that exalteth itself against the knowledge of God, and bringing into captivity every thought to the obedience of Christ. (2 Corinthians 10:5, KJV)

PRAYER FOR ANGER

Father, we are filled with joy that we can come to You. You are a good and perfect Father. Your words are true and can be trusted as the truth. Thank You for the precious blood of Jesus that washes away all of our sins, mistakes, and accidents. Thank You for guiding our footsteps, minds, and actions as we intercede for _____ (grieving loved one). Thank You for knowing the thoughts and plans You have for _____ (grieving loved one). Thank You that Your thoughts and ways are not harmful to _____ (grieving loved one). Please help us to see this, remember this, and walk in faith according to this.

Thank You for sending the Holy Spirit to search our hearts. Thank You that He intercedes for _____ (grieving loved one) in accordance with Your will. Help us to be slow to anger as we walk along this journey. Help us to trust the truth, that Your children have available to them the same power that raised Jesus from the dead. Help us to be strong and courageous as we cast down every imagination that raises up against Your infallible Word. Help _____ (grieving loved one) and me to see those thoughts, emotions, and things that attempt to draw us away from being obedient to You. Thank You that all this is done in the mighty Name of Jesus.

Amen

Guilt

Most guilt, as mine did, develops out of the grieving person's inability to keep their loved one alive. It can be related to many different factors, ranging from childhood experiences to survivor's guilt. The most important element for you to remember is that guilt, along with feelings of being responsible for the death, is common, especially with those whose children have passed over. Guilt can only be validated in a healthy way under the guidance of the Holy Spirit. There are numerous factors that twist and turn through the muddy waters of blame. You must lean hard on God to help your grieving loved one accept, integrate, and move forward past these feelings.

Journey Patterns

1. Exhaustion: Your grieving loved one is struggling to understand their emotions and feelings from one moment to the next. The energy it takes to move back and forth from anger to denial and then to guilt will require all the strength your grieving loved one has. Provide opportunities and suggestions to rest. Yoga, sitting in the park, meditation on God's Word, and reading inspiring books are just a few suggestions. Although the battles are being fought in the heart and mind, the body is where the fatigue will present itself. It is okay. This season will soon pass also.

2. Preoccupation with circumstances surrounding the loss: Your grieving loved one might continually discuss or rehearse the events of that day. I can

remember dissecting the last conversation I had with Michela to the point of recording it. Over the first few months of her death I was also extremely preoccupied with the autopsy, another very common early characteristic of questioning. There was nothing anyone could do to pull me away from my obsession. But questioning is okay, especially in the case of sudden or traumatic losses. The Holy Spirit is there, right in the middle of the work to be done. Offer gentle alternatives in the exact language and dialogue your grieving loved one needs. Trust the Holy Spirit and silently pray. Just because words are not being spoken does not mean the Holy Spirit is not working. The most meaningful conversation right now is between your grieving loved one's heart and the Master Comforter. Trust the truth.

3. Isolation: Your grieving loved one might begin to pull away from family and friends. When you do speak with them or see them, their words, actions, or emotions might seem to be going a mile a minute. Just as with dealing with the anger-based isolation, you might have to work a little harder or be a little firm here. Continue to provide comfort by gently reminding your grieving loved one, "Rejoice in the Lord always. I will say it again: Rejoice!" (Philippians 4:4, NIV). Isolation makes fertile ground for feelings of victimization, such as "no one understands," or "everyone has forgotten or moved on."

These types of words are true signs during grief-related guilt. Continue to use the **Principles** as you walk in the fruit of the Spirit. You will have to be long-suffering and forgiving during this season as well. Remember that your grieving loved one is grieving.

4. Overuse to cope: Your grieving loved one might over-exercise, overwork, and/or use alcohol to drown out or silence the voices of guilt. Feelings of guilt are heavy crosses to carry. Guilt is not only heavy, it also loves isolation. Once again, it is through your watchful observation and prayer that the Holy Spirit is allowing you to witness healthy and unhealthy coping strategies. Seek opportunities to suggest healthier solutions. If your grieving loved one is coping by over-exercising to the point of minor injuries, you could suggest a light stroll in a park with benches to stop and feed ducks. Instead of wearing tennis shoes and jogging pants, you could show up in nice walking sandals. Allow your presence and outfit to give a more relaxed feel. Each time you see a bench or duck, stop and rest. Even though your grieving loved one is still moving, it is not as intense, which is exactly what you are seeking: a gentle redirecting of the behavior. You don't want to come off as attacking your grieving loved one or their unhealthy coping skill. Rather, you are just gently offering better solutions

that will eventually loosen your grieving loved one's unhealthy habit. This is a time during which you will have to be intimately involved and patient. Remember, you are not a professional, and if at any time you feel like seeking help, it is completely okay.

APPLICATION

Apply all four **Principles** here: **Principle 1:** The work belongs to God, **Principle 2:** Silence is more than okay, it is vital, **Principle 3:** The Holy Spirit is the master teacher, and **Principle 4:** The journey belongs to your grieving loved one. Allow these **Principles** to pull you more and more toward your ultimate goal through prayer and supplication as you quietly observe to ensure your grieving loved one does not require professional intervention. If no professional attention is required, continue your position of interceding and not intervening.

Remember, you can trust the truth. It is during these times of wrestling with guilt and feeling exhaustion that your grieving loved one's heart and mind will hear the clear and concise voice of the Holy Spirit. Pray in the Spirit. Fast, if your body allows. If you speak in tongues, speak in accordance with your gifts from God. Jesus gives His disciples a good example of this in Mark 9:29 (KJV): "And he said unto them, this kind can come forth by nothing, but by prayer and fasting."

TRUTH TO TRUST

- Casting down imaginations, and every high thing that exalteth itself against the knowledge of God, and bringing into captivity every thought to the obedience of Christ. (2 Corinthians 10:5, KJV)
- For God has not given us a spirit of fear and timidity, but of power, love, and self-discipline. (2 Timothy 1:7, NLT)
- Pray without ceasing. (1 Thessalonians 5:17, KJV)
- Finally, brethren, whatsoever things are true, whatsoever things are honest, whatsoever things are just, whatsoever things are pure, whatsoever things are lovely, whatsoever things are of good report; if there be any virtue, and if there be any praise, think on these things. (Philippians 4:8, KJV)
- Every valley shall be filled, and every mountain and hill shall be brought low; and the crooked shall be made straight, and the rough ways shall be made smooth. (Luke 3:5, KJV)
- Looking unto Jesus the author and finisher of our faith; who for the joy that was set before him endured the cross, despising the shame, and is set down at the right hand of the throne of God. (Hebrews 12:2, KJV)
- To appoint unto them that mourn in Zion, to give unto them beauty for ashes, the oil of joy for

mourning, the garment of praise for the spirit of heaviness; that they might be called trees of righteousness, the planting of the Lord, that he might be glorified. (Isaiah 61:3, KJV)

Prayer for Guilt

Heavenly Father, we come to Your omnipresent, omnipotent, and omniscient Self on behalf of _____(grieving loved one). "After this manner therefore pray ye:

Our Father which art in heaven, Hallowed be thy name.

Thy kingdom come. Thy will be done in earth, as it is in heaven.

Give us this day our daily bread.

And forgive us our debts, as we forgive our debtors.

And lead us not into temptation, but deliver us from evil. For thine is the kingdom, and the power, and the glory, for ever. Amen" (Luke 11:9–13

Sorrow and Depression

This stage is one of the most universal stages or phases your grieving loved one will experience. It is also the one your grieving loved one will routinely blend with other stages and phases, although in terms of diagnosis it might be difficult. The Word of God gives those seeking comfort explicit instructions on how to put on a garment of praise. As you quietly support your grieving loved one, remember it is less important to diagnose than it is to be vigilant and present in order to know when things are too out of balance. Complicated grief occurs when natural symptoms of grief persist for an extended period of time, or when the actions, words, or behaviors of your grieving loved one threaten the safety of anyone, including themselves or you. It is always better to err on the side of wisdom than to second guess your discerning spirit. This stage or phase, as with all the stages and phases, is temporarily permissible and will pass.

Journey Patterns

1. Exhaustion: Your grieving loved one is struggling to understand their emotions and feelings from one moment to another. This is mentally exhausting. Mental exhaustion can be just as draining to the body as physical exhaustion. If it's true that a body in motion remains in motion, the opposite must be equally as true concerning a body at rest. Extreme sadness places the body's will in a state of rest. The desire or need to do anything can become overwhelming. Even the simplest of tasks, like getting out of bed, can seem difficult. Your grieving loved one might be unwilling to do the necessary physical things they once enjoyed. Begin to incorporate opportunities and suggestions that will get them moving, such as yoga, a walk in the park, or a late-night

swim. Although exercise might be resisted, it is the best way to release endorphins that act as natural antidepressants. Although battles are being fought in the heart and mind, the body is and can be helpful in the fight. Do not demand or force opportunities. The best way is to model the behaviors you are suggesting, such as saying things like, "I am taking my dog for a walk, would you like to join?" or, "The YMCA by your house is my favorite. May I stop by at noon to pick you up?" These are not considered to be demands. They are gentle suggestions in which you are included and intimately committed.

2. Weeping, sobbing, or deep yearning: You will see an amount of tears that are more than just a drop or two, before, during, or after conversations or remembering. The tears pour from a place deep within your grieving loved one's soul. The outward expression of sorrow through tears is the most common release for hurt and pain. Women and girls tend to be better at this than men. For male grievers, you may have to gently say, "It is okay to cry," or "Tears are cleansing," to elicit the response. Encourage them to cry whenever needed. During seasons of deep mourning, you might be here often. It is completely common and healthy to cry.

3. Lack of weeping, sobbing, or deep yearning: The absence of tears or emotions when they seem more

Sharing the Weight of Grief

than warranted may also occur. The release of trauma through weeping, sobbing, or deep yearning is common, but remember, there is no one size fits all. Remember that your grieving loved one does not have the strength to learn or apply new coping skills on a dime. Therefore, those already-learned, normal and natural coping skills will undoubtedly be utilized in times of immediate need. Various environmental factors, family dynamics, and even levels of spiritual belief, as well as cultural norms (i.e. men do not cry), may cause differences in your grieving loved one's journey to and through grief. All emotions, feelings, and actions, or lack of such, are temporarily permissible if no one is in harm's way, including you.

4. Isolation: Men are more likely to isolate themselves and their emotions, but women may do this as well. Your grieving loved one may begin to pull away from family and friends. You may hear them crying in a bedroom, or in a bathroom at work. Isolation is the enemy's attempt to pull us away from those who know their prayers are effectual. Listen for certain clue words, such as "I feel like everyone has moved on," or "No one understands." These are great indicators of potential isolation. Just as with anger- and guilt-based isolation, you may have to work a little harder or be a little firm here. Nevertheless, this, too, shall pass away. It is important to

remember that isolation makes fertile ground for feelings of victimization. Continue to use the **Principles** as you walk in the fruit of the Spirit. You will have to be kind and comforting during this season. Remember, your grieving loved one's heart is being repaired by the Master Physician. Trust the truth.

5. Overuse to cope: Your grieving loved one may over-exercise, overwork, and/or use alcohol to drown out or silence the voices of sorrow and depression. If your grieving loved one refuses to engage for months and is unwilling to stop their unhealthy overuses, you will have to seek professional assistance. As a committed supporter, you must be ready to stand and fight physically and spiritually for your grieving loved one. This might mean coming up against the very one you have been sent to help. This is never our goal, yet we also can never allow anyone to hurt themselves or others. It is important to remember that this is not your journey. You are instead like Simon, selected from the crowd to assist. If a time comes where you are ill-equipped or uncertain, seeking help is always an option. It is okay to temporarily need assistance to cope. Remember that you can trust the truth. Intercede, not intervene. The exhaustion that comes from wrestling back and forth will create space and quietness for your grieving loved one's heart and mind to hear the clear and concise voice of the Holy Spirit.

Pray in the Spirit. Fast if your body allows. If you speak in tongues, speak in accordance to your gifts from God. Jesus gave His disciples a good example of this in Mark 9:29 (KJV): "And he said unto them, this kind can come forth by nothing, but by prayer and fasting."

APPLICATION

Apply all four **Principles** here, which, by this time in your journey supporting the weight of your grieving loved one, should be becoming your first nature: **Principle 1:** The work belongs to God, **Principle 2:** Silence is more than okay, it is vital, **Principle 3:** The Holy Spirit is the master teacher, and **Principle 4:** The journey belongs to your grieving loved one. Allow these **Principles** to pull you more and more toward your ultimate goal through prayer and supplication as you quietly observe to ensure your grieving loved one does not require professional intervention. If no professional attention is required, continue your posture of interceding and not intervening.

TRUTH TO TRUST

- Therefore the redeemed of the Lord shall return, and come with singing unto Zion; and everlasting joy shall be upon their head: they shall obtain gladness and joy; and sorrow and mourning shall flee away. (Isaiah 51:11, KJV)

- But who am I, and what is my people, that we should be able to offer so willingly after this sort? for all things come of thee, and of thine own have we given thee. (1 Chronicles 29:14, KJV)
- My brethren, count it all joy when ye fall into divers temptations; knowing this, that the trying of your faith worketh patience. (James 1:2–3, KJV)
- Likewise the Spirit also helpeth our infirmities: for we know not what we should pray for as we ought: but the Spirit itself maketh intercession for us with groanings which cannot be uttered. And he that searcheth the hearts knoweth what is the mind of the Spirit, because he maketh intercession for the saints according to the will of God. (Romans 8:26–27, KJV)
- For God hath not given us the spirit of fear; but of power, and of love, and of a sound mind. (2 Timothy 1:7, KJV)
- Pleasant words are as a honeycomb, sweet to the soul, and health to the bones. (Proverbs 16:24, KJV)
- Howbeit this kind goeth not out but by prayer and fasting. (Matthew 17:21, KJV)

PRAYER FOR SORROW AND DEPRESSION

Father, we come to You as little children, thanking You for Your goodness and love for us, thanking You for hearing

Sharing the Weight of Grief

the cries of Your children, and thanking You for cleansing us and allowing us the privilege to call on Your Holy Name. We come before You on behalf of all those who mourn and who are suffering from the weight of loss.

We come to You requesting a special prayer for _____(grieving loved one). We stand on Your Word, which declares that the redeemed of the Lord shall return and come with singing unto Zion. We request for Your everlasting joy to be upon _____(grieving loved one's) head, that they shall obtain gladness and joy. We bind sorrow and mourning, as they must flee.

We know You are the great I Am, and all things come from Thee. Thank You for sending the Holy Spirit to help our infirmities as He makes intercession. Thank You for searching _____ (grieving loved one's) heart and being a mighty Comforter. Help _____ (grieving loved one) to receive pleasant words as honeycomb, sweet to the soul. Help us to put on the walk and trust in the truths concerning receiving beauty and garments of praise. Help us to trust in the fruit of the Spirit as we never cease from praying and fasting as instructed in Your Word.

We proclaim victory over every thought which attempts to exalt itself above You. We proclaim love and rejoice in the new things You are doing and will do in _____ (grieving loved one's) life. We trust You with the journey, as

Your will is being done in all of our lives. In the Name of Jesus, the Prince of Peace, we pray.

Amen

Acceptance

When your grieving loved one first begins to accept their new reality, many of the past stages and phases will attempt to creep back up. Continue to trust the truth you have come to master. Your grieving loved one's eyes are being opened as the Holy Spirit is having His perfect way in the daily conversations within their hearts and minds. And while the enemy lays waiting for an opportunity to steal, kill, and destroy what only God can create, Jesus has come that we may have life (John 10:10). Therefore, we rejoice as we begin to experience positive signs of acceptance, never ceasing from praying as well as putting on the whole armor of God. Spiritual battles are a fact of life for the believer. However, we can trust this truth: "Many are the afflictions of the righteous, but the Lord delivereth him out of them all" (Psalm 34:19, KJV). We continue to position ourselves as interceders, not interveners. We continue to apply the **Principles** that we have come to master in a unique and perfect way. We begin to prepare for the celebration as your grieving loved one begins to accept or accepts their physical reality through the guidance of the Holy Spirit.

Journey Patterns

1. Sign 1: You will begin to witness your grieving loved one trusting in the truth more. They will begin to realize that it was wrong that their loved one was murdered, or died by suicide, or was taken from them too soon, but that God can still use it for good. "And we know that all things work together for good to them that love God, to them who are the called according to his purpose" (Romans 8:28, KJV). This is what you will begin to see represented in the words and actions of your grieving loved one. It might sound strange at first. Their words and actions might not completely align. I would write scriptures on the palm of my hand or on note cards and rehearse them whenever I felt waves of emotion rising up inside of me. I would speak them over myself. I understood in my head that God's Word was true, and my heart, with its hope so long deferred, was starting to receive it as well.

2. Sign 2: You will begin to witness your grieving loved one have a deeper appreciation of the value of God in their life. It might seem to be too much at first. During the early stage of acceptance in my life, my friends and family thought I lived at church and Bible study. I listened to Bible apps and YouTube videos of sermons all day, and even while I slept. The value of spending time with God overshadowed all

other desires. Eventually, circumstances balanced out, allowing me to stand without the intentional and deliberate isolation of all else except the Word. The message here is not to worry about or doubt the form of your loved one's acceptance, but rather to allow the process you have come to master to continue to have its perfect way.

APPLICATION

Apply all four **Principles** here: **Principle 1:** The work belongs to God, **Principle 2:** Silence is more than okay, it is vital, **Principle 3:** The Holy Spirit is the master teacher, and **Principle 4:** The journey belongs to your grieving loved one. Allow these **Principles** to pull you more and more toward your ultimate goal through prayer and supplication as you quietly observe to safeguard the good fruit of your grieving loved one's newfound acceptance. Remember that you can trust the truth, and to intercede, not intervene.

TRUTH TO TRUST

- For the weapons of our warfare are not carnal, but mighty through God to the pulling down of strongholds. (2 Corinthians 10:4, KJV)
- For by him were all things created, that are in heaven, and that are in earth, visible and invisible, whether they be thrones, or dominions, or

principalities, or powers: all things were created by him, and for him. (Colossians 1:16, KJV)

- Though he slay me, yet will I trust in him: but I will maintain mine own ways before him. (Job 13:15, KJV)
- Who shall separate us from the love of Christ? Shall tribulation, or distress, or persecution, or famine, or nakedness, or peril, or sword? (Romans 8:35, KJV)
- So shall my word be that goeth forth out of my mouth: it shall not return unto me void, but it shall accomplish that which I please, and it shall prosper in the thing whereto I sent it. (Isaiah 55:11, KJV)
- O sing unto the Lord a new song: sing unto the Lord, all the earth. (Psalms 96:1, KJV)
- For the mind set on the flesh is death, but the mind set on the Spirit is life and peace. (Romans 8:6, NASB)

Prayer for Acceptance

Our great and wonderful Father: Oh, how we love to acknowledge You. We come before You because You have been faithful and are deserving of all our praise. Thank You for guiding our footsteps as we intercede on behalf of all those who are mourning. Thank You for giving _____(grieving loved one) hope and a newly discovered acceptance of and dependence on You. Thank You for weapons of warfare which we have come to trust are not carnal, but mighty through God to the pulling down of strongholds. Thank You for delivering _____ (grieving loved one) to a point of acceptance concerning all grief-based strongholds.

Thank You that nothing can separate _____ (grieving loved one) from the love of Christ. Thank You for Your continued guidance and protection from the tribulations, distresses, persecutions, famines, nakedness, perils, and swords which will surely attempt to steal, kill, and destroy the promises in which _____(grieving loved one) has come to trust.

Help _____ (grieving loved one) to remember and trust that the Word of God which comes forth out of his/her mouth will never return void, but shall accomplish and prosper as You have sent and purposed it. Give _____ (grieving loved one) a new song to sing to You today, a new song of unwavering acceptance and reliance on You.

We trust You and accept the truth concerning our earthly mindsets of death, and place them captive under the mindset of the Spirit which is life and peace. It is in the power of the precious blood of Immanuel in which we pray.

Amen

Engaging in Life

We have arrived at the purposeful position we have been seeking for so long. The colors which seemed to be all black and white for so long have dissipated, and now we can see and smell and savor the promises of God. This is when most believers find the strategically positioned treasures, passions, and purposes that were hidden within the constraints, pressures, trials, and tribulations of the journey. Breath now returns to its home, and your grieving loved one has the muscles to stand stronger than ever against the stages of grief. Although as children of God we do not ignore the presence of evil and evildoers in this world, we do rejoice in the victory and finished work of Jesus on the cross.

The principles of this book have allowed you to never cease from praying for your grieving loved one. Your intimate work with your grieving loved one has revealed to you many closely kept truths about them over time—and now it is time for you to encourage them to stand firm in God's truth without your assistance. Just as with most strategies and tools, it is always better to wean yourself slowly. Remember, helping your loved one achieve total reliance on God and reach this stage has always been your ultimate goal. While, like a good parent whose child leaves for college, it can be a very difficult and prayerful transition, nevertheless, there is still more good news . . .

JOURNEY PATTERNS

1. Matured sign 1: Trusting the truth is now your grieving loved one's first response. They are completely sold out on the truth: "And we know that all things work together for good to them that love God, to them who are the called according to his purpose" (Romans 8:28, KJV). Clarity is here! You will rarely ever hear or see evidence of their old grief perspective. All evidence points to and validates the completed work of God's Word accomplishing that which pleases God.

2. Matured sign 2: You witness your grieving loved one daily experiencing a deeper appreciation of the value of God in their life. The perfect, completed work of the Holy Spirit is here! Your grieving loved one will attend church because they desire to be in the house of the Lord, not because it is the only way they can find weekly peace. They now enter into God's gates with thanksgiving and praise, adding to the celebration as they rejoice. As they rejoice, their balance has returned, and now they are more capable of providing help to others.

3. Relinquishing previous patterns: All temporarily permissible signs, such as isolation, weeping, exhaustion, outbursts of despair, overuses to cope, and questioning, have been brought under submission. Your grieving loved one's trust in the truth and

appreciation of God provides a bulwark against all other stages and phases which dare to stand against the infallible Word of God. As supporters, we must remain as diligent, approved scholars of the Word and never cease from praying, as the expectation we have been purposefully awaiting has indeed arrived.

Application

Apply all four **Principles** here: **Principle 1:** The work belongs to God, **Principle 2:** Silence is more than okay, it is vital, **Principle 3:** The Holy Spirit is the master teacher, and **Principle 4:** The journey belongs to your grieving loved one. We have been so quiet over this process; now would be a great time to shout "Hallelujah!"

Truth to Trust

- Being confident of this very thing, that he which hath begun a good work in you will perform it until the day of Jesus Christ. (Philippians 1:6, KJV)
- Be careful not to practice your righteousness in front of others to be seen by them. If you do, you will have no reward from your Father in heaven. (Matthew 6:1, NIV)
- Casting down imaginations, and every high thing that exalteth itself against the knowledge of God,

and bringing into captivity every thought to the obedience of Christ. (2 Corinthians 10:5, KJV)

- If it be possible, as much as lieth in you, live peaceably with all men. (Romans 12:18, KJV)
- And thou, Solomon my son, know thou the God of thy father, and serve him with a perfect heart and with a willing mind: for the Lord searcheth all hearts, and understandeth all the imaginations of the thoughts: if thou seek him, he will be found of thee; but if thou forsake him, he will cast thee off for ever. (1 Chronicles 28:9, KJV)
- The Lord shall laugh at [the wicked]: for he seeth that his day is coming. (Psalm 37:13, KJV)
- God is our refuge and strength, a very present help in trouble. (Psalm 46:1, ESV)
- Who shall separate us from the love of Christ? Shall tribulation, or distress, or persecution, or famine, or nakedness, or peril, or sword? As it is written, for thy sake we are killed all the day long; we are accounted as sheep for the slaughter. Nay, in all these things we are more than conquerors through him that loved us. For I am persuaded, that neither death, nor life, nor angels, nor principalities, nor powers, nor things present, nor things to come, nor height, nor depth, nor any other creature, shall be

- able to separate us from the love of God, which is in Christ Jesus our Lord. (Romans 8:35–39, KJV)
- My brethren, count it all joy when ye fall into divers temptations; knowing this, that the trying of your faith worketh patience. (James 1:2–3, KJV)
- In all thy ways acknowledge him, and he shall direct thy paths. (Proverbs 3:6, KJV)
- And we know that all things work together for good to them that love God, to them who are the called according to his purpose. (Romans 8:28, KJV)
- So shall my word be that goeth forth out of my mouth: it shall not return unto me void, but it shall accomplish that which I please, and it shall prosper in the thing whereto I sent it. (Isaiah 55:11, KJV)
- Rejoice in the Lord always. I will say it again: Rejoice! (Philippians 4:4, NIV)

Prayer for Engaging in Life

Father, we are so very thankful and grateful that Your words toward Your children are true. Thank You for being with us through this journey. Thank You for the sanctifying blood of Jesus. Thank You that _____(grieving loved one) is confident that You perform all good works until the day of Jesus Christ. Thank You for restoring _____(grieving loved one's) peace. Thank You for protecting and preserving _____(grieving loved one's) mind with Your perfect placement of his/her helmet of salvation. Thank You for protecting _____ (grieving loved one's) heart and vital organs with his/her breastplate of righteousness. Thank You for hiding Your Word in _____(grieving loved one's) heart and infusing it in his/her mind, as it is a two-edged sword allowing him/her to cut through bone and marrow. Thank You for increasing _____(grieving loved one's) faith, which shields him/her from the fiery darts of the enemy, including the stages and phases of the grief he/she has left behind. Thank You that we have grown stronger in Your truth, which girts up all loins. Thank You that _____(grieving loved one) is fully persuaded that nothing can separate him/her from Your eternal love as he/she begins to sing a new song. Thank You for keeping _____(grieving loved one's) feet shod with the preparation of the Gospel as he/she pursues the land of the living. Thank You for being _____(grieving loved one's) refuge and strength, a very present help in trouble.

Amen

References

Albuquerque, S., Pereira, M., & Narciso, I. (2016). Couple's Relationship After the Death of a Child: A Systematic Review. *Journal of Child & Family Studies, 25*(1), 30–53. https://doi.org/10.1007/s10826-015-0219-2

Alonso-Llácer, L., Barreto Martín, P., Ramos-Campos, M., Mesa-Gresa, P., Lacomba-Trejo, L., & Pérez-Marín, M. (2020). Mindfulness and grief: The MADED program mindfulness for the acceptance of pain and emotions in grief. *Psicooncologia, 17*(1), 105–116. https://doi.org/10.5209/psic.68244

Becker, C., Clark, E., DeSpelder, L. A., Dawes, J., Ellershaw, J., Howarth, G., Kellehear, A., Kumar, S., Monroe, B., O'Connor, P., Oliviere, D., Relf, M., Rosenberg, J., Rowling, L., Silverman, P., & Wilkie, D. J. (2014). A Call to Action: An IWG Charter for A Public Health Approach to Dying, Death, and Loss. *Omega: Journal of Death & Dying, 69*(4), 401–420. https://doi.org/10.2190/OM.69.4.d

Finnäs, F., Rostila, M., & Saarela, J. (2018). Divorce and parity progression following the death of a child: A register-based study from Finland. *Population Studies*, *72*(1), 41–51. https://doi.org/10.1080/00324728.2017.1337918

Iglewicz, A., Shear, M. K., Reynolds, C. F., Simon, N., Lebowitz, B., Zisook, S., & Reynolds, C. F., 3rd. (2020). Complicated grief therapy for clinicians: An evidence-based protocol for mental health practice. *Depression & Anxiety (1091-4269)*, *37*(1), 90–98. https://doi.org/10.1002/da.22965

Malgaroli, M., Maccallum, F., & Bonanno, G. A. (2018). Symptoms of persistent complex bereavement disorder, depression, and PTSD in a conjugally bereaved sample: a network analysis. *Psychological Medicine*, *48*(14), 2439–2448. https://doi.org/10.1017/S0033291718001769

Nielsen, M. K., Neergaard, M. A., Jensen, A. B., Vedsted, P., Bro, F., & Guldin, M.-B. (2017). Predictors of Complicated Grief and Depression in Bereaved Caregivers: A Nationwide Prospective Cohort Study. *Journal of Pain & Symptom Management*, *53*(3), 540–550. https://doi.org/10.1016/j.jpainsymman.2016.09.013

Ott, C. H. (2003). The Impact of Complicated Grief on Mental and Physical Health at Various Points in the Bereavement Process. *Death Studies*, *27*(3), 249. https://doi.org/10.1080/07481180302887

Robinson, T., & Marwit, S. (2006). An Investigation of the Relationship of Personality, Coping, and Grief Intensity

Among Bereaved Mothers. *Death Studies, 30*(7), 677–696. https://doi.org/10.1080/07481180600776093

Scott, H. R., Pitman, A., Kozhuharova, P., & Lloyd-Evans, B. (2020). A systematic review of studies describing the influence of informal social support on psychological wellbeing in people bereaved by sudden or violent causes of death. *BMC Psychiatry, 20*(1), 1–20. https://doi.org/10.1186/s12888-020-02639-4

Tal, I., Mauro, C., Reynolds III, C. F., Shear, M. K., Simon, N., Lebowitz, B., Skritskaya, N., Wang, Y., Qiu, X., Iglewicz, A., Glorioso, D., Avanzino, J., Wetherell, J. L., Karp, J. F., Robinaugh, D., & Zisook, S. (2017). Complicated grief after suicide bereavement and other causes of death. *Death Studies, 41*(5), 267–275. https://doi.org/10.1080/07481187.2016.1265028

BIBLE REFERENCES

Scriptures marked ESV are taken from English Standard Version®. Copyright © 2001 by Crossway, a publishing ministry of Good News Publishers. All rights reserved.

Scriptures marked GNT are taken from the Good News Translation® — Second Edition. Copyright © 1992 by American Bible Society. All rights reserved.

Scriptures marked HNV are taken from the Hebrew Names Version. Public domain.

Scriptures marked ISV are taken from The Holy Bible: International Standard Version. Release 2.0, Build 2015.02.09. Copyright © 1995-2014 by ISV Foundation. All rights reserved internationally. Used by permission of Davidson Press, LLC.

Scriptures marked KJV are taken from the Holy Bible, King James Version. All rights reserved.

Scriptures marked NASB are taken from the New American Standard Bible®. Copyright © 1960, 1962, 1963, 1968, 1971, 1972, 1973, 1975, 1977, 1995 by The Lockman Foundation. Used by permission.

Scriptures marked NIV are taken from the New International Version®. Copyright © 1973, 1978, 1984, 2011 by Biblica, Inc.™. All rights reserved.

Scriptures marked NKJV are taken from the New King James Version®. Copyright © 1982 by Thomas Nelson. All rights reserved.

Scriptures marked NLT are taken from the New Living Translation®. Copyright © 1996, 2004, 2007, 2013 by Tyndale House Foundation. All rights reserved.

About the Author

Dr. Jacqueline L. Phelps is a subject matter expert with over eighteen years on her own grief journey. She has completed over five hundred hours of extensive training as a grief facilitator and annually commits to professional development endeavors such as conferences, symposiums, and subject matter interviews related to the stages and phases of grief.

Dr. Phelps is a biblical scholar and lover of knowledge. Whether a student of theology or secular research, she considers herself a lifetime learner. A gifted communicator with a unique delivery style capable of crossing gender, age, and cultural barriers, Dr. Phelps loves people and building relationships.

Dr. Phelps's professional diversity ranges from health and research to academia and instructional design. *Sharing the Weight of Grief* combines Dr. Phelps's life experience, professional diversity, and spiritual truths.

CREATING DISTINCTIVE BOOKS WITH INTENTIONAL RESULTS

We're a collaborative group of creative masterminds with a mission to produce high-quality books to position you for monumental success in the marketplace.

Our professional team of writers, editors, designers, and marketing strategists work closely together to ensure that every detail of your book is a clear representation of the message in your writing.

Want to know more?
Write to us at info@publishyourgift.com
or call (888) 949-6228

Discover great books, exclusive offers, and more at
www.PublishYourGift.com

Connect with us on social media

@publishyourgift

www.ingramcontent.com/pod-product-compliance
Lightning Source LLC
Chambersburg PA
CBHW072000070526
44583CB00015B/1270